May these words fall as blessings

With My Last Breath, I'd Say

I Love You

*xo
Shauna*

With My Last Breath, I'd Say

I Love You

When Your **Faith** and **Hope** Slip, **Grace** Wins Every Time

Shelley Taylor

Carpenter's Son Publishing

With My Last Breath, I'd Say I Love You

©2018 by Shelley Taylor

Published by Carpenter's Son Publishing, Franklin, Tennessee

Published in association with Larry Carpenter of Christian Book Services, LLC
www.christianbookservices.com

Cover and Interior Design by Suzanne Lawing

Edited by Tammy Kling

Copy Edit by Christy Callahan

Printed in the United States of America

978-1-946889-19-5

Stories of Hope

Acknowledgments

Taylor and David, you've both encouraged my writing daily, and I am forever indebted to you both.

Taylor, you've encouraged me longer than anyone and kept telling me how important this book was, and that I need to get to "The End." After Mother died and I said, "I don't think I can do the book. I don't think I can finish it," you said, "Mom, you didn't teach me to quit! You aren't quitting now." I'll never be able to tell you how much those words meant to me.

David, you encouraged me to write nightly and made it seem possible that I could finish. You complete me and make me know we're a team, and I'm forever grateful for your support. You were God sent, and your words pierce my heart with just the right amount of love. You both are the perfect mixture of love and grace when I doubted myself and thought publishing this book wasn't possible. It wouldn't have been possible without the two of you!

Claire J. De Boer, your words have helped heal me and have touched me beyond any words of gratitude that I could ever write. Words fail me here, truly. I am grateful for your strength to write healing words. Your words paved the way for mine, and I am forever grateful to you for sharing them.

Shauna Niequist, you put a pencil to my soul. It's no mistake that our lives crossed paths exactly when they did. I read your books *Cold Tangerine* and *Bittersweet* both during some of the saddest times of my life and you helped dry my tears and turn them into words that I pray are helping others.

Claire and Shauna, you both are my writing mentors and I can't explain how much your words have meant to me.

From My Heart to Yours
A Letter to the Reader

Let us not become weary in doing good, for at the proper time we reap a harvest if we do not give up. —Galatians 6:9

Tears drip down my cheek while I slowly twirl a ringlet into a tangle. There's irony in a beautiful curl slowly turning into a tangled mess, beyond resurrection, in a matter of minutes. The words "He brought me to it, He'll bring me through it" play over and over in my head. Writing has been the one thing to bring me so much joy, and now it provides me utter frustration. "Am I still able to link words?" I'd often asked myself, and this time would prove to be no different. I didn't seek to be a writer; words found me years ago, yet they seem so far away. In 2010 my life turned disastrous in seconds, just like the curl—everything a tangled mess.

What mattered the most to me before seems hugely insignificant now, and the little things that I typically overlooked daily became huge! In that moment, God began rewriting the ending to my life's story, our worlds collided with His, and He provided us with the most beautiful second chance. My daughter and I were poisoned by carbon monoxide, and the night fell short of us drawing our last breaths while sleeping. Our lives were forever altered: we both began to get migraines, and my breathing, memory, and balance (just to name a few) changed in the blink of an eye. We are now survivors, not victims of traumatic brain injuries. Every day is a constant reminder that He interrupts our lives and it's ok to embrace imperfection.

Writing would forever be a challenge. I would have to dig deep within myself to the places He had already nestled and cling to them. He landed on us and brought our focus off the things that didn't matter and onto the little things that do. Even as I write these very words, I wipe constant tears. The struggle is relentless and oftentimes paralyzing. Yet I continue to embrace the big and small moments—every breath I'm given. So often my faith and hope slip, but grace wins every time. Today is one of those days; I recall words as they come, thankful that no one is here seeing the pain. Even more thankful that I am sitting here breathing breaths while my heart beats. Sometimes the lack of negative memories is nothing short of God's grace and mercy. If you are reading this, it's only by God's grace that this book was written and published.

One night I lay in bed, thinking how far I'd come, how far my sisters and I had come through the years: "I have a brain injury, I'm a daughter of a prescription drug addict, I'm divorced." Then I burst into tears, rejoicing. "I'm a survivor! I'm a daughter of a King! We are daughters of a King! My sisters and I survived!"

Our lives are not lived without struggle, chaos, and defeat. Each season changes us and He does this with intent. Things don't happen without purpose, without reason. These seasons and events don't take Him by surprise, though they may surprise us. These seasons encourage us to seek Him. You may feel as if you are drowning by a recent struggle. But let Him steady you, let Him sustain you. Whether He gives you the opportunity to suffer, big or small, believe in Him and in His promises. He has a plan specially created just for you. For every inhale and every exhale, breathe Him in. So many days are met with great struggle, but I try my best to remember He chose this life for me. I am a part of His plan; how can I ever doubt Him? He knew the breaths that would follow me would bring great challenge; He knew this, He knew.

It was not by mistake that my mother became an addict, for it's by this that I believe I am who I am today, and my sisters are who they are. Our daughters are strong and courageous women because of the lives we lived and the lives we've lived with them. Over the years my heart ached for the addict my mother had become, and that night God placed on my heart to do what I had learned, what was comfortable—write about it. This book is a biological postcard to our mother, a rite of passage, so to speak. It's been a huge part of my healing—each word bringing me closer to the end, each word sparking the dry kindling in my chest, each word connecting to the next as if a flame on dry grass.

I just wanted to go from victim to healed, and this was my way to do that. I didn't want to wake up with the taste of regret. I would heal through writing, and my words could heal others. What happened in between the voices, between the unspoken words—that's what I wanted to write. That's the story I wanted to tell. I want you to be there, with us, between the breaths, between the heartbeats, between the words spoken and not.

I pray this book, in its naked honesty, honors her by bringing others hope during times of desperation. My sisters and I made it through, and so can you.

Writing is my therapeutic outlet, and when I connect my fingers with the keyboard, my soul bleeds and I become raw and honest, discovering who I was and who I truly am. Some days writing is my soft place to fall and other days I cannot even stand afterwards. It's hard to understand how pain can be both fierce and numbing at the same time. Writing has been my refuge. It is the backbone to my courage on many days.

I write love letters back to the Lord, praising Him for all He's done for me. I am one of those people who believes everything happens for a reason. I know people say that in jest, but I truly believe this with everything I am. We lived! We are survivors, not victims. This book is intended to remove the veil of our life, and my desire is that our transparency will resonate with you and help heal you where you are broken.

My *hope* is that you, the reader, will be *encouraged* by who we are and by the breaths we have taken both in brokenness and in bravery.

God puts us in people's lives and puts people in our lives to change us. Our reactions and choices put steps in place to form us and those who are intermingled with us. You'll hear me say later that sometimes the story isn't even about us; we are just His vessels to help orchestrate His plan. What an honor. I hope by the end of this book, you are stronger than when you began and you will allow Him to use you in His great orchestration. I truly wouldn't change who I am because it was those breaths and heartbeats that made me the person brave enough to link these words. God knew all along the choices that I would make. Who am I to want to have lived a different life or alter His plan? He knew all the things He would put at my feet, and He knew how strong they would make me. I truly believe we can't change what He lays at our feet, but we can let it change us. We can allow it to break us or make us; I chose the latter.

This book is my story, but I'm sure it's also someone else's as well, it may even be yours. It's anyone's story who needs help and hope to deal with what God has put in their path. It's a book of great hardship, great faith, and His grace. There is a light at the end of the tunnel. God can use our sadness as His finest hour!

I wrote every word to encourage you. I wanted to write a book that I could've picked up when tears dripped down my cheek and words of hope would have helped me along. I want this to prove that even in our darkest hours, He is there to give you encouragement to endure the battles you face. No matter what He puts at your feet—abuse, cancer, death, financial difficulties, unemployment, infidelity, divorce, sickness, unplanned pregnancy, singleness, infertility, a wayward child, depression, anxiety, loneliness—He is there! No matter what season you are in, joy or weeping, He does not forsake His children, so find Him in each season. No one is perfect, but His grace covers all our sins, and He's washed me in His mercy too many times to count.

Every experience has truly been worth it. My hope is that my pen has as much ink as the ocean, my fingers can continue to type, and I can continue to write all the days that He chooses to let me be here. I wonder if I will ever have written out all of the pain? If I don't, it's ok as that's what made me who I am. I can't imagine living any other life, as all the good and all the bad has led me here. I spent many, many nights waking up to a word or sentence that had to be written. I write life. I write to connect with you. If I had lived a life that was painless, I wouldn't have needed to write this book and I would've missed the opportunity to connect with you. I write to voice my pain so maybe your faith can grow stronger by what I've lived.

I'm slow and meticulous in taking steps forward (one foot in front of the other). I gladly celebrate each step I take. I stop to smell the roses, and the places I go, I go with intention. I don't want to celebrate when I get there; I want to celebrate life as I go, living with wild abandon! I don't want to find Jesus when I arrive, but I want to have taken Him on my journey. Lord knows that I will fall along the way, literally and figuratively, but I will pick myself up and begin again with one foot in front of the other.

So many *wonderful* things happen when
you just begin with one step or one breath.

Try it. What do you have to lose? Let Him support you, let His grace break your fall. You may have been slowly turned or vigorously thrown by the storms of life, but you are still usable bent or broken, beautiful or tangled. He will put you back together if you give him the chance.

What's *tangled* in your life?
What will you allow Him to untangle?

You can do it; I know you can! If you need support, encouragement, or a nudge, you've got it! God's love for us is huge and gentle at the same time. His love is as intentional as are our trials and hurts; they're not mistakes to Him. He may not move your mountain, and He may even allow a larger one to stand before you, but He will walk the path with you if you let Him. If you've lost your trust in Him, if you feel broken and helpless, if you're drowning, over your head in despair, in need of just one more breath, this book is for you.

With my last breath, I'd say I love you.

❤

Lord, please let these words land on those who need them.
*Even if it's just one, Lord, may this book encourage that **one**.*
Amen.

From my heart to yours:

We have all struggled just trying to reach His hem. Sometimes He lets us grasp only a thread and sometimes He engulfs us in His Robe. His grace is there for the taking.

My prayer for you, the reader:

I pray this book is a "cozy fire" experience, not a roaring blaze, to both heal you and hold you. Let this book be both a flashlight to a glimpse of hope and a softly struck match in your darkness. May you be both lost and found in my story and feel the warmth engulf you while learning from our experiences.

His healing words to your heart:

"Let us then approach God's throne of grace with confidence, so that we may receive mercy and find grace to help us in our time of need" (Hebrews 4:16).

Introduction:
Our Story of Poisoning and Grace

But he said to me, "My grace is sufficient for you, my power is made perfect in weakness." Therefore, I will boast all the more gladly about my weaknesses, so that Christ's power may rest on me. —2 Corinthians 12:9

I must not only believe in Him and in His promises, but if I am given the "opportunity" to suffer, what will I do with this opportunity? So many days are challenging and bring a stream of tears, but I try my best (and often fail) to remember that He knows the plans for me and for my daughter, Taylor. Through it all—truly through it all—I will trust Him, and I'm forever grateful that she's learned to trust Him too.

In the blink of an eye, so many memories were gone, wonderful memories and not so wonderful memories.

I wish I could've chosen the ones that stayed and the ones that left. So many beautiful moments have been taken away and horrible ones remain. If I could trade them, I would, but I know the memories that remain are what make me who I am today. I'd be a different person right now if I didn't retain some of the things I lived as a child and as a young adult.

There are days that will change everything. We had one of those days, and it would turn into a complete game changer. A day we will never, ever forget. A day I've documented in words with the intention that if the day comes that the memory is gone, I can always reflect back on His goodness and mercy. The night we were poisoned was the night our worlds collided with His and He provided the most beautiful second chance.

The snow had been falling for days, and we were experiencing a rare "Texas winter," and had received about six inches of snow in the preceding two days. The power had been off, and we had no idea when it would come back on. On day three, we ran a generator out in the front driveway/edge of our garage with the garage door open and the windows in the garage open, trying to provide some type of power to sustain us until the electric company could repair the outage. We went to bed all bundled up, trying to stay warm until the power came back.

Taylor woke suddenly to what she thought was someone screaming her name! She jolted up in bed, tried to stand, and quickly realized that her legs wouldn't hold her up. Then she fell to the floor, army-crawled across the floor to her door, and again tried to stand. She was too dizzy and collapsed again, all the while having the feeling of tunnel vision where you can't really hear or see. It was frightening! I heard her body crash. I knew something was wrong and I went running. Charlie (my ex-husband and Taylor's dad) heard this as well from the living room, and he and I met at her doorway and found her lying lifeless face down on the floor.

It is the worst feeling to stare at your lifeless child and not know what is wrong and not be able to see enough in the darkness to assess the situation. Charlie tried to prop her up, but no matter what we did, she was unresponsive. We kept asking her what was wrong and to wake up, but we got nothing. She wasn't responding and my heart sank. Charlie was shaking her and trying to get a response. He frantically sent me to get the flashlight on my nightstand. We were both beside ourselves, lost in this moment of not knowing, this moment of terror. On my way to the bedroom, the effects of what was happening to Taylor began happening to me. I started feeling like I was losing control, and as the time slowed and seconds passed, I knew I had to get to Charlie to let him know something was seriously wrong with me. I just didn't know what!

I had the flashlight in my hand and started running back to the hall, but the closer I got to him, the farther away it seemed. Everything spun out of control and I lost awareness of where I was. I knew if I didn't make it back to him, he wouldn't know to come find me. I was experiencing the worst feelings I had ever faced. As I focused on just making it back to them, I turned the corner to the hallway and collapsed face first. Without any hands or arms to brace myself, I fell onto the metal flashlight, cutting my forehead open and exposing the bone underneath. Charlie searched in the dark for the flashlight as it had rolled when I fell, and I tried to tell him I felt blood running down my face. Things were completely out of control at this point. Once he found the flashlight, with one look he said, "We have to get you to the hospital!" My reply: "What is wrong with Taylor? Doesn't she need to go?"

Somehow in my head and my heart, I wasn't thinking about me. I was thinking about my daughter and how her fall had alerted us to this whole ordeal. Meanwhile, Taylor was in and out of consciousness. Charlie was able to wake Taylor for a few moments and told her to get a towel to help with the bleeding until help arrived. My head began to pulse blood out of control, and soon Taylor and the walls and I were all covered in blood. How she made it to the bathroom and back with a towel is beyond any of our comprehension. She immediately passed out again after she handed Charlie the towel, not far from me. Charlie dragged her over and propped her on top of me, against the wall, and I began having convulsions and banging my face into the floor. My eyes were rolling back in my head, and Charlie was yelling at me, "You aren't going to die on me!"

Charlie called 911, and the police were the first to arrive. Upon entering, they looked for the lights, and Charlie told them we were still without power. Using their flashlights, the first sight they saw was all the blood—bloody handprints in our hallway where I tried to stand and blood covering Charlie and Taylor as well. Immediately they began accusing him of a crime, and to anyone just entering the situation, it certainly didn't look good. He began explaining what had just transpired.

Shortly thereafter, the fire department arrived, and luckily Charlie knew one of the firemen, who quickly came to his defense, and changed the perspective of what was going on. The fire chief began asking questions as to what we had done earlier in the day to try to figure out what happened and puzzle out the problem. Charlie told him about the generator use, and the chief darted to the truck to get the carbon monoxide detector.

The truck was parked out in the street, and within steps of entering our driveway, the readings on the detector began to rise quickly, so much that the chief went back to the truck to recalibrate the device because he just couldn't believe that the high readings he was getting so far from the inside of the house could be accurate. Once again as he walked in the driveway up to our front door, the readings began to creep higher and higher. Upon reaching the door, he called for his crew to exit the home and began to get Charlie, Taylor, and our dogs out as well. You could see by his expression that he was very concerned about the safety of this environment and what was happening, not only for us but for his crew.

Only a couple of paramedics were left inside to stabilize me for transport to the hospital. Once outside, they realized that this whole incident had begun with Taylor's episodes of unconsciousness, and the firemen told Charlie they wanted her checked out at the hospital as well. I left by ambulance, and Charlie drove Taylor in his truck. The fire chief later told us that since it was so cold and there was no wind, the gas probably just settled instead of blowing away and crept back into the house via the eaves.

En route to the hospital, through nothing other than God's grace and strength, Taylor made some of the scariest and bravest phone calls she's ever made. She called my sisters to let them know what happened and told them to come as quickly as they could, with one sister coming from hours away.

She was much too young to understand the depth of what was going on or what was wrong with her mom, but I believe she feared for my life and she knew they had to get there quickly! Several firemen stayed at our home to open windows and watch our dogs for sickness, making sure they were in a safe place before leaving—way beyond the call of duty. Once we arrived at Mansfield Methodist Hospital, medical personnel checked my and Taylor's blood gases, which were "through the roof," hers being much higher than mine. At that time, they were not prepared or skilled to handle emergencies such as ours, and they began preparing us to be transported to Dallas Methodist Hospital to get in their hyperbaric chamber.

Before they could transport us, they had to stitch me up. After fifteen stitches and a CT scan, it was determined that I was safe to transport. Off Taylor and I went in the ambulance, driving across ice, her sitting strapped in and me on a stretcher, both of us with oxygen on and both terrified.

Somewhere along the way, my oxygen ran out and the face

mask adhered to my face, and being claustrophobic, I began to quickly panic. The paramedics were wonderful and helped me get it off and continued to race as quickly as we could. When we arrived at Dallas Methodist Hospital, a doctor explained the procedures for going into the hyperbaric chamber. Meanwhile, the carbon monoxide was still doing internal damage to our bodies and brains. I was just trying to follow along and understand what was happening the best I could! During the explanation, why he felt the need to tell us this, I'll never know, but he explained that the family that had just been in the chamber all died, except the father. This gave us more stress and fear as to what was coming next. I was terrified for Taylor, I was terrified for me: Was she going to be ok? Were we going to die?

Taylor and I are both very claustrophobic, but we pushed through our approximate three-hour stay in the hyperbaric chamber! (Taylor was such a trooper, as they had a very difficult time getting her to the required depth to be successful. Her experience was much worse than mine.) To this day, she says she will never go back in the chamber, and I hope she is never challenged with that decision. Two ambulance rides, one CT scan, two blood gases, two hyperbaric chambers, fifteen stitches, two brain injuries, and one concussion later, we survived! Nothing says I love you like a brain injury on Valentine's Day.

When we arrived home from the hospital, I grabbed Taylor's forearms and said to her, "You know the voice that woke you up was not me or Daddy?" Her response: "I know, Mom!" My faith is amazing and God's mercy is incredible!

After all that happened, my sister Kimberley (Kim later in life wanted to be called Kimberley, but most of the time she's still Kim to me) moved in for about a month to help me heal mentally and physically, as well as help with Taylor and the necessities around our home. Physically I was still healing from my head wound and mentally I was left with a traumatic brain injury. I felt like I was starting over as a kindergartener. I literally started my recovery with kindergarten flashcards, looking at an apple and saying library. Kimberley quizzed me over and over with the flashcards and always encouraged me when the wrong response came out. She was a godsend. My friends, coworkers, and family completed most of my sentences, and they scooped Taylor and me up and helped us heal.

My neurologist told me that people don't survive what we went through, and there really aren't patients like us. "We really don't know how to treat you."

I cried, looking at him and seeing that he was visibly shaken. Through his honesty, he became a great comforter to me as I struggled with memory and cognitive skills. We became a little closer that day, and I knew he had chosen the right career. We agreed that Taylor and I were living on a wing and a prayer, and for that we were and remain truly grateful for God's grace and mercy and all the incredible people He has placed in our path. I was treated by this doctor for about a year and a half, trying to find something that would help.

At one of my first visits, he made a fist and began knocking on my forehead. "The poison goes into your brain and destroys whatever it attaches to," he said. "We have no control over what functions it destroys or limits. We just have to push forward and keep doing our best and see what each day holds for recovery."

God is the God of *miracles*.

My short-term memory is horrible at times, and I've lost so many precious memories from both my long-term and short-term memory. Taylor and I have a saying when it comes to trying to remember things: we just look at each other, and one of us will say, "Did we have fun?" The one who remembers says to the other, "Yes, we had fun!" That's all that matters. To be alive, in whatever capacity, is amazing! God is good—no, great! His grace is unending!

I continue daily to deal with migraines and challenges with my balance, breathing, vision, and memory (or lack thereof). These are daily struggles for both Taylor and me; this is our reality. I have fallen more times than I've stood it seems, sustaining injuries that ranged from Band-Aids to orthopedic visits. For six years, my greatest challenge was breathing, but now I struggle with a chronic migraine. (As I wrote this, I was over two hundred days straight of my head hurting.)

Every day, at some point I struggle to breathe, and coughing has become my norm. Some days are better than others. Sunny days are my friend, yet I lean on Him for every breath I take on cold, wet days. The more I talk, the worse my coughing gets, and I talk so much for the work I do. Recovery continues every day for me and Taylor. Luckily her dyslexic brain is used to accommodating skills, and this continues to be her saving grace on a daily basis. She is young and strong, and her faith is incredible. Healing has come differently for her, but memory, migraines, and sleeping issues are big battles for her that she faces with amazing courage on a daily basis. As you read this, I'd love for you to pray for her right now. May God always pour His grace and peace out when it seems the suffering has no end.

I could never thank Taylor enough for her bravery that day. I wish I could've held her hand while we were in the hyperbaric chamber, but I was in mine and it was not possible. To see her struggle that day made my heart sick. I am grateful for each day we have together and all we will have in eternity. Little did we know that we were moments from not waking up and dying from carbon monoxide poisoning. Every breath we take is a reminder that we live. Not everyone who goes through something like this survives. Some never get the chance to live like we were, and we are truly grateful.

Then they cried to the Lord in their trouble, and he saved them from their distress. He sent out his word and healed them; he rescued them from the grave. Let them give thanks to the Lord for his unfailing love and his wonderful deeds for mankind. —Psalm 107:19–21

God used this disaster to dissolve a broken marriage and link my life with the most amazing man, through merging tears, broken hope, and many answered prayers. Never did I think that David would be my reward. Spending the rest of my life with him is truly a dream come true. I am beyond blessed. I pray that we never take for granted what God did and never forget that most people never survive what we went through.

❤

Thank you, God, for giving me a second chance at life! I will not take it for granted, and won't let You down. I'll spend every day giving You the glory!

From my heart to yours:
- Even in your storm, where can you give Him the glory?
- God is a God of second chances. Do you give others a second chance?

My prayer for you:
I pray that when your world changes in a breath, in that split second, that no matter the circumstance, you will praise Him. And if He allows you a second chance at life and doesn't bring you home, use it to His glory!

His healing words to your heart:

"You hem me in behind and before, and you lay your hand upon me" (Psalm 139:5).

Chapter 1:

Embarrassment versus Necessity

Those who look to him are radiant; their faces are never covered with shame. —*Psalm 34:5*

Life gives us many opportunities to share our stories. My and my sisters' story is so embarrassing to tell, but it's too important to those it could help not to. It's uncomfortable alone when your story involves an alcoholic and prescription drug addict. The discomfort takes on a new level when that person is your mother. She's the one who gave me life and the one who, in other moments, made me feel as if my heart would stop beating.

Our life was tenderness turned tragedy. It took grit to endure, but sometimes grace is given in grit and determination. Addiction levels the playing field. It doesn't discriminate, as with anything He sets in our path. We have common breaths thread through pain that have linked the threads of endearment between us, and we now include you, the reader.

Let His *faithfulness* destroy your doubt. And even if
you hang on by a tiny drop of hope, hang on.

To be completely candid, after my mother died, I thought
my heart would "shift." I thought her death would change how
I felt. It didn't, and I was hurting. Our mom died December of
2014 and so did the chance to change her. The chance to have
that little girl's fairy tale of having a mom who was my best
friend, who shared more than the blood that ran through our
veins. The realization that we can only change ourselves never
dulled the pain of not being able to reach her. I will breathe
my last breath sprinkling joy and providing hope to those who
suffer.

I want you to *know* and *believe* in His grace.
You aren't alone.

I am so grateful God does not forsake His children in their
deepest need—whatever that looks like in your life: addiction,
cancer, abuse, divorce, death, finances, job loss, singleness,
unplanned pregnancy, etc. I hold to the thought of all the children who are bound by the common denominator of a non-
present parent. It is deeply saddening. I am not angry but sad,
and I know I am certainly not alone.

He *knows* our stories.

I'm a risk manager and, well, I manage risks. Everyone's
appetite for risk is different as are our abilities to handle the
battles and challenges He puts before us. What may be nothing to me may be huge to you. My nothing and your every-

thing are all equal to Him and handled the same in His eyes. My "daughter of a drug addict" may be "cancer patient" or "single mom" to you. If it's big to me and big to you, then it's big to Him. Together we can make it through by helping ease each other's loads. Thank you for coming along on my journey, I hope it lessens the challenge of some of your breaths.

Words heal. Sometimes the lesson's hard. Oftentimes the lesson hurts. Life hurts when God allows hard things to come our way. Sometimes we become our best teachers, if we will allow ourselves to learn from our experiences, both the good and the bad. I believe God puts us just where we are supposed to be, and sometimes the lesson is not even meant for us. What you go through may be for someone who God chooses to cross our path in one way or another, and we must learn to be His vessels. I pray that you'll let Him use you.

Let your "hard" *soften* you. Let Him *mold* you.

I totally believe that I am who I am and my sisters are who they are because of the things He laid in our path. God gave me the best two sisters I could've asked for to live and breathe out these experiences with, and I couldn't imagine if either one were missing. Kimberley and Courtney are the kind of people you want with you in the trenches, and they proved that. God must have always known that we were stronger than we appeared, as we are here to tell our story. Gratefully, many times I have told myself that He doesn't just pick anyone to suffer like we have. It is both humbling and honoring to know that He can use us to help others, and by this we can help ourselves. We individually bled from the same place, our hearts. We bent, we broke, and we survived. We are seekers of God's grace and have lived both horrible and beautiful moments from which we share. I am overjoyed you're here, and I hope we can connect in your beautiful or broken place. I am so grateful that His mercy mends the broken.

He knows the story of every tear.

You keep track of all my sorrows. You have collected all my tears in your bottle. You have recorded each one in your book.
—Psalm 56:8 NLT

Some days just connecting breaths is a struggle and I want them to be worth it. I want every breath I breathe to be worth the breath. The journey ahead is getting shorter every day, and I want every step I take to matter. Every step takes me closer to the end, and after losing both parents, this has hit closer to home. No matter who you are, you only get one life to make a difference—make it count. Everything we have and every day we are given is a gift from God. Everything, period. Every breath you breathe, the one you just exhaled. Live with intention and give Him the glory.

I want to make a difference because I was here. A legacy of hope and love that lasts. I can only hope that at the end of the day, at the end of the final breath I take, that I have made a difference to someone, that I provided a light in someone's darkness.

It's not too early or too late to think about the impact you make and it's certainly not too late to change or strengthen your legacy. Even on your lowliest of days, you are who you are for a reason and no one else is uniquely you.

Fill yourself with what you want to leave behind.

Our stories define who we are, and connect us with those who have walked similar paths. Connections are so beautiful if you know the Connector. Whatever you are dealing with right now, you can rest assured someone else has lived and made it through, and so can you. We grow from each other's experiences. When that someone puts their arms around you, pulls you in tightly and says, "I've been there," let your fears and tears mix with theirs.

❤

Lord, I pray You lead me to the pain and help me help You mend the broken. God, we can't change what You put at our feet, but we can let it make us instead of break us. Hard will always come. I pray You soften us by what You allow us to endure.

From my heart to yours:

- What's *your* story? Is it too embarrassing to voice?
- Think of those you influence, you inspire. What legacy will you leave?
- How can you allow God to use you? How can you be *His* voice?

My prayer for you:

Thank you, God, for the silent ones, the ones that only You know. Pull them in close today, close enough to hear their hearts beat and feel their breath. God, use us, each one who is taking the time to read these words.

His healing words to your heart:

"You, Lord, keep my lamp burning; my God turns my darkness into light" (Psalm 18:28).

Chapter 2:
Debutante to Addict

Charm is deceptive, and beauty is fleeting; but a woman who fears the Lord is to be praised. —Proverbs 31:30

We were born to one of the classiest women around, as we were daughters of a debutante. Mother's parents divorced when she was a little girl, and she lived with her dad. Mother was born into a wealthy family with nannies and caregivers to make sure she had the finest of everything. She was a daddy's girl, and he denied her nothing. Nothing was too good for his baby girl. She always got her way. Our mom was a princess.

A master at manipulation, Mother lived and died knowing she would get things her way. Unfortunately, her dad and our grandfather lost his fight with cancer when Mother was a teenager, and none of us received the chance to know him. Nevertheless, his French blood flows through my veins, and I'm reminded of him when I look into a mirror and see my dark hair and dark eyes.

Mother and Dadi were connected by a mutual friend who knew they shared a lot of things in common. It was love at first sight for Dadi, and he, without hesitation, knew he would marry her. Our parents' marriage lasted one hundred and twelve days' shy of fifty-six years. No one on this earth would or could doubt our Dadi's love for our Mother.

Our Mother was stunning! She was a beautiful, slim woman, with dark, striking features, who made men turn their heads without hesitation. I can recall a picture of her during her college years where she had a striking resemblance to Jackie O., and Dadi always thought she looked like but was more beautiful than Elizabeth Taylor. Her figure was such that at the time of my birth you could barely tell she was pregnant. Back then Mother had friends, purpose, and character.

When I think about her, two memories I have are her sitting on top of her bed, her back against the headboard and Nanny (Mother's mother) laying in front of her and Mother plucking Nanny's eyebrows. I know you are probably thinking this is odd to tell, but my mother did this a lot for her, and it's one of the only two compassionate memories I have of her. The other is that Mother always called me "love"—something I carried on with Taylor. Through the years, I have called Taylor "love" instead of her name.

Though I am sure there are others, be it my memory issues or just plain forgetfulness, these are the only things I can remember about Mother. She had many amazing and positive titles when we were little girls: Girl Scout Leader, room mom, gardener, craft enthusiast, bridge player, German shepherd breeder, horse lover, barrel racer, church volunteer, golfer, beach lover, mother, friend, and wife.

During the time we lived in Acton, Texas (a small town outside of Granbury), Mother was very active at church; she also played golf and worked tirelessly in our garden that was an acre in size. Mother had a very caring heart, and it was important to her to share the food from our garden. Mother was a "cowgirl" and she "broke" horses for people. For those who don't know what this is, in layman's terms, Mother took the unruliest horse and made it to where it could be trusted even with a child on its back. She was active, she had tenacity and she loved being outside. We had horses that she tended to daily, and she was normal. Acton is where I began riding horses daily and that is where my love for them began. Our family did things together—fun things—and the life we experienced was no different than any other little girls. When we were small, she was still beautiful inside and out, and we were a family. Destruction had not yet knocked on our door.

It was after our move to Mansfield in 1974 that her looks, her life, and the lives of her children would begin to be altered. "Country club to chaos" comes to mind. Mansfield was a small town, quiet and quaint, and I often wondered who, besides us, knew that Mother had a drinking problem. Sitting here now, looking back, I know we weren't alone. I can remember now some of the other women, moms that lived lush, luxurious lives that also fit in her category, wondering now what happened to them and their families. Mother had friends that she drank with, golfed with, and smoked with and such, and friends that began to see her change. Friends that questioned her behaviors and those who didn't. This was the beginning of a very difficult season for us as Mother began to drown and medicate her emptiness.

We saw her begin to change during this time in our lives. It was a gradual change, nothing that just happened overnight. Each day she became less and less of the wife our dad had wed and less and less of the Mother we knew. Days were both exhilarating and exhausting, and this continued into adulthood. Each day we lost her just a bit more, and my separation from her began. Children are taught to step back from the flame as to not get hurt, and I can still feel the heat.

Mother continued to stuff whatever was hurting her deep down inside. With her continued decline, I began a pattern that would last a lifetime; when forced to choose between fight or flight, I chose flight.

Every waking hour when not in school, I either rode horses, fished, golfed, or played tennis. I stayed busy and kept my mind occupied. I told my deepest feelings to my horse while riding bareback. The only things between me and her bare back were the secrets we shared. I can still remember propping up against her chest, escaping in books and doing homework.

Looking at her life now, all the things we've been through and experienced, that was probably the best time we had with her. It was the best it would ever be for us. I was in fifth grade. At that time, at least Mother was a functioning alcoholic and still engaging with people, sober or not.

If Mother put makeup on, it always consisted of scarlet lipstick, perfectly blotted with a piece of tissue. If she was seen with makeup, she probably was leaving the house, with no concern as to what she had ingested. Mother often didn't think of others and the risks she was taking on the roads prior to driving on them.

I still wonder where she bought her alcohol. Did I go with her? Did Dadi buy it for her? I never saw it come into the house; I just saw bottles that she tried to hide.

I was taught to drive by a drunk. It was on a trip with her that I was forced to learn to drive at the mere age of twelve. The alcohol had once again consumed her, and she chose to leave the house, getting behind the wheel and endangering both her life and mine and everyone else on the road.

We were going across the bridge on Hwy 287 and I-20 about to break the barrier that held us safely in the lane when I screamed, "Pull the car over or I'll jump!" I opened the door and she stopped the car immediately. Luckily, I had many "driving lessons" while closely watching what she did as I knew someday this same scenario would happen. I had played it out many times, in my mind, while pressing my lips together as tightly as I could and keeping myself from screaming "Stop!"

I exhaled a pinned-up breath. None of these times, knowing she terrified me, ever bothered or concerned her; she just smiled at me with her scarlet lips. So many times, it was never about me, and only about her. I wanted so badly for her to love us recklessly. Instead, her actions were reckless. Why wouldn't she let Him quench her thirst? Mother went to the wrong well.

"Come, everyone who thirsts,
come to the waters." —Isaiah 55:1 ESV

Mother painted manipulation, pain, distance, selfishness, and sadness with broad brushstrokes all over her children. Emotional abuse goes further and deeper than neglect. It is typically a choice one makes—intentional, willful. Mother inflicted irreparable damage upon her children and her husband and continued to do so without remorse. It's only by God's grace that we are the encouragers we are today. Sometimes one should learn by example, not live by it.

There are so many things that Mother did and was that I hope and pray I never am. When I hear women say, "We are turning into our mothers," I cringe with the thought. We were tiny gifts from God that she had been given the privilege and the duty of raising and nurturing, and it felt as if we were not worthy of her love. We were tainted, marked, scarred with the ugliness that we lived in. We were surrounded by wrongdoing, wrong choices, and bad behavior. Sin!

We were left to fend for ourselves. We learned to take care of each other, to love, and to have compassion, honor, and kindness and bestow these things on others. We learned it despite the example that we were given.

We learned to be who we wanted *her* to be but she wasn't! We learned to carry on while we had Mother's shards of pain in our sides. Mother masked her pains with medications and alcohol and didn't care how her children were hurting. She never realized that what she was doing to herself had a direct impact on us. Until the day she died, Mother stayed in a constant state of numb.

Mother's personality took a nose dive from extrovert to introvert; she no longer engaged, she retreated (I'm sure from the drugs she ingested). I have no memories of Mother being drunk for long periods of time. When she drank, she drank until pure drunkenness and then went to her room to sleep it off behind a locked door. When Mother was passed out, there was no waking her. We were abandoned, neglected within our home. Dadi missed so much of this as he left early for work and came home late, probably for a reason that was never voiced but seems so obvious now. Possibly he simply couldn't watch what was happening.

Mother controlled our house from inside her locked bedroom. On occasion, Kimberley would try to wake Mother up to get lunch money. Numerous times, Courtney and I tried to wake her as well, screaming, "Mother! Mother!" and "Angelyn" to no avail, while shaking her violently thinking, "I'm dead if she *does* wake up."

Right now, I can remember thinking there was a fine line between waking her and her being upset, and needing her and not being able to wake her. We began leaving the screen off their bedroom window and the window unlocked so we could climb in to check on her. Mother found out that this was how we gained access to her, and she began locking the window.

Tears fell with reckless abandon. Could she not hear her daughters' cries? Could she not hear the tears fall from our faces? Her drunkenness was so severe that hardly anything woke her when she was passed out. If you could wake her at all, she would come up swinging, yelling, "Leave me alone," or just making sounds, moans that couldn't be interpreted. I can hear them still right now in my head. Kimberley began just getting her lunch money out of Mother's purse, and Courtney and I just left her room feeling defeated.

Mother had edges that were sharp, that cut even those closest to her. She "dictated" what she could as her means of maintaining control, including using her "white glove method" of checking our assigned housework. I have memories of a poster board with our names and assignments listed, but never really any memories of Mother cleaning with us. If you failed the white glove test, you started over and over until she approved. (Later in life when we had housekeepers, one lost her job as she would spray Pledge in the room, and not actually clean, and Mother would not stand for that.)

For me and my sisters, part of getting a driver's license included being handed the sale ads from the newspapers. Our job was to purchase groceries that Mother had circled and the exact quantity she had written from numerous stores, and if they were out of that item, you had to always get a raincheck. We drove to Skaggs, Eckerd's, and other stores in numerous towns to get the "bargains" Mother had selected. This was always very important to her: 1) that we do it and 2) that we do it right.

Somewhere along the way, Mother lost her hope, she lost her faith, she lost our names.

> *I lift up my eyes to the mountains - where does my*
> *help come from? My help comes from the Lord,*
> *the Maker of heaven and earth. —Psalm 121:14*

There had been so many pills taken, drinks consumed, strokes suffered, and heart damage done that she continued to mix up the names of her daughters and granddaughters in most every conversation spoken. It would make sense that she not know our names because at best she had sketchy relationships with us and our girls. Taylor, and especially Kelsey, feel as if they didn't have a grandmother. It is sad but very accurate. Why would they have had a grandmother? I didn't have a mother. It makes sense that she would not retain any maternal patterns once she was lost to her addictions.

Mother missed so many things along the way, me being crowned Miss Mansfield and Homecoming Queen, Friday night football games with me cheering, and any other school function. (Kim videotaped the pageant, and I guess we showed it to Mother later as she was in rehab, again, but I'm not sure she ever watched. Dadi drove me to other pageants and modeling jobs, and Mother was nowhere in sight.

One of the angriest moments of my life was when she missed Charlie's (my ex-husband) mother's funeral! She and Dadi drove from Texas to Oklahoma, but Mother made him get her a motel room along the way as she "just couldn't make it" as she said her pain was too bad and she couldn't ride in the car any longer. I was furious. We were stressed beyond belief from a week-long ordeal of his mother's attempted suicide and subsequent death. *She was miserable?* We were all miserable from what we had dealt with, our hearts were broken, and I was too exhausted to be as angry as I should've been. Even in this time of crisis, my own mother couldn't support us. Charlie's mother always supported me and I loved her deeply! We had not slept in four days. Our heads literally had not hit a pillow. We brushed our teeth in the sink of the public restroom wearing clothes we had worn for days, and I was still suffering the effects of a concussion sustained weeks earlier. As always, Mother's drugs took precedence. It should have come as no surprise.

Charlie's mother took her own life because she felt she

wasn't good enough and in that sadness, she felt no one cared. In that moment, she was right about my mother. She didn't care. To this day it is sad, inexcusable, and embarrassing.

Courtney by far had the closest and longest relationship with Mother. That closeness has made it very, very hard for her since Mother's death. I continue to pray so many prayers for her hurting heart as I know she loved and felt loved differently than I did.

Reading and writing were luxuries that Mother didn't possess any longer. It was especially sad to us as Mother used to love to read and told us books would take us places. So much damage had been done to her cognitively because she went against the advice she gave us and used drugs to get away. We took her advice and used books to "go" places, and she used drugs to "escape" places.

It is because of a birthday card that I received from Mother and Dadi one year that I began writing OXOX often instead of XOXO. Mother signed my card and wrote, "OXOXQQQ? Q?" I have no idea why a Q, but my thought is that it looks closest to the O and there was that cognitive confusion. Oftentimes Dadi just signed her name instead of going to the trouble of her trying to sign her own. The deep sadness of this sticks in my mind. To sign a card took great concentration from her, and then it was almost illegible. Years and years ago, Mother was known for her penmanship. She had very articulate writing that she was very proud of that mirrored the strip of letters that lined the top of the walls in an elementary classroom. Mother was a different person then. It was things like this that both sickened me and broke my heart at the same time. Where did that mother go?

Once beautiful, she started spending her days in an old tattered T-shirt with more burnt cigarette holes than not, and this was fine with her. If I had seen my Mother on the street, I would've thought she was homeless. (Come to think of it,

she was "home" less, *we* were "home" less and "homesick." I
could no longer find my Mother's face in this woman, in this
stranger. Pictures of her showed an empty, sad, hollow woman
with slim, withered, and frail legs protruding from her white
granny panties, asleep or better spoken, passed out. Her legs,
unsure of their next step, continued to hold her up even when
we couldn't until the day her body said enough is enough.
As she continued to deteriorate, Mother forever walked with
a limp, dragging one leg behind. The right side of her body
stopped working, and she became frail, weak, and in need of
constant care and attention of both her walker and Dadi.

Being right-handed, she learned to eat and do tasks with
her left. Mostly she just decided to do nothing for herself and
let it be done either by an aide or Dadi, or things were simply
not done.

*My flesh and my heart may fail, but God is the strength of my
heart and my portion forever. —Psalm 73:26*

Even in her broken condition, she still thought of herself
as a princess and wanted everything her way. I can recall the
time we took Kim to Outback Steakhouse for her birthday; it
was a rare opportunity for Mother to be in the presence of all
her girls. Instead of finding joy in us all being together, Mother
ordered her "own" blooming onion so she didn't have to share
with her children. Point proven and I was forty-eight years
old. I pray that someday when I or we walk into Outback, the
memory and sting will have lessened. Mothers should hold
the family together, but mixed with alcohol and drugs, they
tear it apart and this proved to be true in my family.

Even in my fifties, I still try to understand the decisions she
made. Some days the pain is unbearable! Endless questions
that hit me at different times. Why can't I get past this? Why
does it matter after all these years? Why did it ever matter?

Why did she always come first? Who could not love their children? "Selfish" and "mothers" should never go together.

She was sad to look at and even sadder to be around. Mother hadn't contributed one thing to the world, community, or anyone in 40 plus years. Mother woke up every morning, sat in her recliner, and fell asleep or passed out there—continuously. Food was brought to her, she used the potty chair right in the middle of the living room, and I was disgusted at the woman she had become. You cannot free someone who doesn't know they are enslaved. You cannot save someone who doesn't want to be saved. You cannot help someone who doesn't want to be helped.

Dear God, where is my Mother? Where is the woman that birthed me? Where is the woman that cared what she looked like and cared what we thought of her? Dignity is far removed from her.

No temptation has overtaken you except what is common to mankind. And God is faithful; he will not let you be tempted beyond what you can bear. But when you are tempted, he will also provide a way out so that you can endure it.
—1 Corinthians 10:13

He will not allow us to be tempted more than we can bear. It doesn't mean He won't allow more problems than we can bear. I believe that He provided Mother an "out" that she just didn't take.

Whether we are beautiful or tainted, fabulous or failing *His love* endures forever.

We can walk away from the cross, our children, and everything Jesus, and He doesn't waver; He doesn't move or falter. No matter how far we wander, we're never beyond the reach of His saving hand.

We can mar or mark this world and the places we go; Mother marred and Dadi marked, for sure. Dadi loved to draw and paint and was an unbelievable artist. He painted the most incredible pictures and probably "escaped" a lot while doing so. Everyone who knew him knew he was very gifted and creative in art.

Dadi lived in filth and painted *beauty*.

Dadi mostly painted breathtaking scenery, probably wishing inside that he was there instead of where he was. He painted and drew pictures of Mother looking beautiful back in the day. I hope in my heart that he still remembered her this way even though right now it is hard for me to remember that person behind all that she became. Where did the stunning woman go?

If Dadi took a chisel and carved away at her, I believe that the woman he married was in there somewhere, but that person was never to be seen again. That person was never to be again. Mother became so far removed from who she once was I don't even know if she remembered her.

A mistake repeated more than once is a decision.
—Paulo Coelho

I know now, as an adult, that Mother decided to live this life. Drugs and alcohol made it easy for her to numb the realization of what she didn't want to face. Still to this day, we can't put our fingers on what went so wrong and what it was that she needed numbing from.

Something was so big to her that she couldn't take it to the One that would easily bear that burden for her. He bore the weight of the cross; He would have gladly carried whatever it was she held.

My sister Kim stepped in or stepped up so many times for me. If the truth be known, after Kim and Billy married, they both acted as my parents. A huge reason that I am who I am today is because of their intervention and her being the "mom" that I needed. Kim rescued me (more than once) and cared for me deeply, then and now. She risked a lot to love me and get me from where I was to where I am and I will never, ever forget that. She pays consequences, even still for the choices I made. Kim has provided an example not only for me, but for her daughter's and mine. She is one of the godliest and selfless women I know.

I thank God for her daily. Truly, thank You, God, for her! When your mother's not there for you and you end up with Kim, you have won—truly you have won—and I don't tell her thank you enough. I am blessed and Taylor is blessed to have had her intercepting in our lives and interceding for us still today.

❤

Thank You, Lord, for all our stories
and for making all our breaths count.

From my heart to yours:
- What in your life has left you feeling like it was complete chaos?

- What do you feel you should step back from because the hurt is too deep?

- What do others see when they look at you?

- What do you see when you look in the mirror?
- What bad choices in your life has God's grace covered?

My prayer for you:

Lord, thank You for loving us through the disasters in our lives. I pray that You provide an extra measure of grace and comfort to make it through and we can live lives worthy of Your honor.

His healing words to your heart:

If we confess our sins, He is faithful and just and will forgive us our sins and purify us from all unrighteousness (1 John 1:9).

Chapter 3:

Learning Who to Be

A generous person will prosper; whoever refreshes others will be refreshed. —Proverbs 11:25

Granny and Gran-Gran (Misty is the eldest great-grand-daughter, and she renamed Gran-Gran to Granner) were our Dadi's parents, and the road we traveled to their house in Cleburne, Texas, was as familiar as the lines on my hand. The trees in their neighborhood were old enough to touch in the middle of the streets, and they did. The sky and the top of the trees met seamlessly, and it was beautiful. We had some amazing times there, and their home is where we learned "family." The backyard was a haven to our swing set, Granny and Gran-Gran's swing, and whatever bird dog made his home there for a while. These dogs may have been trained and taught to retrieve bloody, wounded, or dead birds back to their own-ers, but when brought back to the house, they were covered in kisses and love from us girls. In our family, dogs are like people and treated as such, then and now.

Their living room appeared huge at the time, and it was our makeshift skating rink. We adorned Gran-Gran's socks, stood at one end of the room, and plunged forward on the shiny, slippery wood floor to the other end. We stood, and began again, back to the other side. Now as an adult, I have learned that this once-appearing huge room was really just a cozy, charming space in their white wood-framed home on Douglas Avenue. We made lots of memories there.

Granny's kitchen not only had the warmth from her stove but the warmth from her heart. This is where I learned to love cooking and recipes and everything food related. Before you were totally awake in the mornings, Granny was at your bedside asking if you wanted your eggs fried or scrambled, biscuits or toast, white or wheat, sausage or bacon. These were really important decisions that we made way too early, and only at her house would this have taken place. My Granny cooked my Gran-Gran breakfast every morning while listening to KCLE (the Cleburne Radio Station) and she brought his coffee to him at the table, where he slurped it from a brown saucer made of pottery. As a little girl, I thought this was so cool, and I couldn't wait until I grew up so I could do it also. Now that he's gone, I can't help but think that he would love that I'm a coffee drinker, and I wish so badly to share a cup with him while talking about bird dogs and barber shops.

Gran-Gran sat in the same seat at the table every time, the same seat in which he counted his money from barbering on Fridays and Saturdays. He organized his bills across the table, and often we got to help him count and straighten them.

Granny taught us so many things about love, marriage, and being a wife. She is how I learned to put myself second and put others before me, and if I burned some food or messed up the recipe, that was what I should eat, not serve. I still remember and adhere to this today, and this is what I taught Taylor as well. My grandparents showed me love, not only between themselves but with us and to us. We didn't lack for anything when we were with them; we were spoiled rotten. Granny and Gran-Gran were your typical grandparents who held the bar high. Granny never entered our front door empty handed; she worked at a boutique and often brought us clothes from market. We had the best clothes!

Every Sunday we either drove to their home to have lunch or they would drive to us, with an entire meal packed ever so gingerly in a box in the trunk. This box was nestled closely to bubbles, coloring books, comic books, and all sorts of smile-making "sussies" (gifts or small tokens). Granny certainly knew how to pack love in a trunk. Then and now we related food with love. Even now when we make "Granny's lasagna" or "Granny's rice," it is associated with the love she brought and all the miles she traveled to do so. With all the chaos in our lives, we knew their love for us ran deep. We never ever doubted that.

I try to remember though it can be hard to reach at times, but I believe we had several years at their house prior to my mother's full-on addiction. However, I think my Granny knew something was odd with our mother long before it was spoken in words.

Days were always filled with fun and sweet memories. We sat in old metal chairs out in their front yard, waving to neighbors and passersby, if we weren't too tired from playing in the sprinkler or climbing the mimosa tree. My grandparents waved to familiar faces and strangers all the same. Life was different then, and the world was a very different place. We slept on cots that were stored above the garage door and fell asleep with Granny rubbing our backs and bottoms.

We knew to listen for the whistle blow to tell hardworking, aged men to begin and end work at the Santa Fe Railroad. Gran-Gran worked for the Santa Fe Railroad as a boiler maker, Monday through Thursday, then as a barber Fridays and Saturdays. Our little hands helped prepare Gran-Gran's lunch that Granny sent with him each day. I can still remember the ham sandwich on white bread, the small bag of Fritos (with the eraser inside), the pink snowball cupcake, the Zero candy bar, and the ice in the small, round Styrofoam container with a lid.

Cleburne, back then, had the best tasting water ever and the best ice! We longed to drink their water. When we opened up Granny's freezer, it always held the popsicles or Italian Ice that we loved. We ate popsicles, Italian Ice, and snow cones until our hands were stained, our bellies were full, and our lips were frozen and colored.

We always went to church with them on Sundays and sometimes sat upstairs in the choir loft with Granny. If not there, we sat in the small soundproof room for crying babies (only because it was a cool place to be) or we sat with Gran-Gran, who would sit by himself if we didn't. He sang softly. We went up front for the children's sermon and learned about Jesus.

After church, we would go back to their house, and Granny would serve us a yummy meal that she began preparing long before we woke, and then we rested before our car ride out by the lake. Gran-Gran always said, "Let's go see if the lake's up or down." We fished often, either on the side of the lake or from Gran-Gran's fishing boat whose home was beside their house, outside the bedroom in which we slept. I did and do love to fish with a Zebco rod and a red-and-white bobber, preferably with a worm or minnow, and the size of the fish doesn't seem to matter as long as the bobber goes under. Occasionally we would go out on the lake and troll with lures, and we ate beanie weenies for lunch with smelly worm-dirt-soiled hands, and oftentimes Dadi went with us. I could take the fish off my hook, but preferred help most of the time. We fished no matter the weather.

I can still see my Gran-Gran in his pale olive-green coveralls and Granny in a house dress of the same color and her sparkly gold slippers with pointed toes. We watched Granny knit, crochet, latch-hook, cross-stitch, or work on some other needlepoint project, and on many occasions, she taught us her art. Sometimes we helped her by threading her needle or organizing her yarn. We colored pictures, and our masterpieces covered their walls. The pieces stayed displayed until the tape turned the color of rust and no longer stuck to the walls. Granny was proud of us and told anyone who would listen all about everything we did, with the truth stretched a little. We learned about our heritage by going to the cemetery and changing out flowers. We hung clothes on the line with wooden clothespins and swung either in the big wooden swing with Granny or on the metal swing set that tipped if you swung too high.

We stayed with Mammaw (Gran-Gran's mother) while Granny worked, and we were always so excited to get to walk to the store or hamburger joint with her leading the way. None of us could keep up and we were often more tired afterwards than her. We prowled around with wonder in her barns and picked pecans from the deep-rooted trees in her yard. We didn't sit on her bed as it had an electric blanket hidden beneath the bedspread and now I wonder why that mattered. She lived in a large triplex and had scary renters each time we visited. We had TV dinners and potato flakes from a box, and drank soda pop out of her fridge.

We sat at her vanity, playing in her makeup and jewelry before and after watching The Lawrence Welk Show. Mammaw sat in her chair while we plucked her whiskers with her tweezers and an old antique mirror. I can still see the Lawrence Welk bubbles and smell Mammaws foundation each time I open up my powder in the mornings. She had a huge porch and swing where we'd sit with her, hot or cold, watching cars drive by. Kimberley remembers listening to Elvis on Mammaw's old Victrola (a vinyl record player/turntable). Mammaw loved us and was a precious God-fearing woman who would've died for us, given the opportunity. Her love was amazing!

She lived almost a hundred years and died of a horrible bout with shingles. I happened to have the misfortune of driving by her home, many years after she was gone, while it was engulfed in flames. I hadn't been to Cleburne in years, and what were the odds that I would be in front of her home the exact moment it was burning down? I believe God was in control of even that moment.

> Tears slid down my face while the firefighters sprayed water on so many *memories*.

Granny was a large lady; however, I didn't look at her and think she was large, but she was most definitely tall and very put together. I looked up to her in so many ways. Her hair was always a beautiful shade of silver and always looked as if she just came from the beauty parlor, and on many occasions, she had. If her hairnet had not performed properly and her hair got out of place when she slept, we girls got to repair the damage. These are beautiful memories that I have. In Granny's home is where I learned to "rat" hair with her rattail comb.

Granny wore fashionable pantsuits and adorned every one with strands of beads and pearls, and I always thought she was so classy. I never had to guess where I got my love for jewelry. She had necklaces and earbobs a plenty.

Granny had a sewing machine and her house was always full of fabrics, yarns, thread, and bobbins that she used for sewing, knitting, crocheting, or cross-stitching, and she taught us anything we wanted to know. She continued sewing even after her eyes failed her, and she couldn't thread a needle without a magnifying glass or the help of our tiny hands. Misty would be the only great-grandchild that would get homemade blankets, smocks, and such. Granny knitted and crocheted constantly while watching TV.

Then while Gran-Gran had his many hospital stays, surgeries, treatments, and dialysis, she would knit or crochet to pass the time. I remember so many times as a teenager driving from Mansfield to Cleburne, picking Gran-Gran up and taking him to Fort Worth for his dialysis treatment. I sat crocheting with her in many a waiting room, and at night in the comfort of Ronald McDonald-type housing in Temple during Gran-Gran's many stays at Scott and White Hospital. People welcomed us into their homes. When I think back now on their kindness, I realize that back then I didn't fully understand the grandness of their gestures.

Granny's home was full of familiar smells. Granny herself had a familiar smell, one that was lovely, and I still can smell it as I type. She worked at a boutique with wood paneling that was sprayed daily with Claire Burke Original Potpourri, and the paneling had taken on its fragrance. Granny told me once that the entire case of potpourri cost seven dollars. I bet you can't buy one can for that now. This smell seeped into her skin, and we cannot smell it without thinking of her. This smell makes me feel safe, at home and loved; it feels as if I am being wrapped in a warm blanket.

I can still see the cases of cans lining the back room. That back room (for workers only) was where us girls added on the adding machine, ringing up "fake" customers on the "tickets" we made up while Granny sold dresses and such to real customers in the other room. I wonder how many rolls of adding machine tape we went through and how many sales pads we wasted. Those are wonderful memories, truly wonderful memories.

Granny was not selfish; she purchased things that we loved.

Granny taught us how to give. She spent her days and nights doing for others. She went out of her way to help others and taught us how to as well. Every Friday, Granny would take money to Dee (a blind man), and we went with her often. My sisters and I are benevolent and give any way we can; it's important to us. My sisters are two of the most benevolent souls I know! Be careful telling them something you love; you will probably end up with it.

Kimberley used this example: if someone comes to your house and comments they love something you have, wait a bit, then gift it to them. You can't take it with you, and you impart love and joy to others in the process. This is most definitely a trait that we learned from Granny, along with so many other beautiful things. There are so many times I do things and know that I learned it from Granny, and I hope that my grandchildren learn beautiful things from me as well.

So many things are contagious. Shouldn't "giving" be one? It's like asking, "Who wants coffee?" at a party, and one responds. Then after smelling the nice aroma, someone says, "Did you make enough for me?" People want what others have.

We travel the roads to Cleburne less often now as God has taken the ones we traveled to home with Him, but the memories are forever in our hearts and souls. Traditions were developed back in the day and are carried out still with our families and friends.

Part of our childhood we lived in a quaint wood-framed house where we shared bedrooms and great times in Acton, Texas (a small community outside of Granbury where we rode the bus to school). This home was our first experience with a claw foot tub. Acton is where we met some incredible people, and their friendships have lasted a lifetime. Some of my fondest "first" church memories came from Acton, and ironically God has nestled my childhood pastor Gary Lindley close by me my entire life, no matter where I have lived.

Gary's compassion and kind words throughout my life meant more than he'll ever know or any words I could ever express. I am forever grateful for the Christian foundation he provided that has lasted my entire lifetime. Gary is one of those people that are in your life that make you know God is good! Acton is where we gardened, painted cookie ornaments for the church bazaar, rode horses, rode minibikes, played golf, swam and fished at De Cordova Bend and Pecan Plantation, and canoed the Brazos river. And it's the first place I ever knew dogs could wear shoes.

Nanny (my mother's mother) had arthritis so badly that her fingers were permanently deformed. Her skin was soft, softer than any I had touched, and her frame was small. She had wrinkles a plenty, too many to count. There was not any skin on Nanny that didn't have lines and creases, and this was always a true fascination of mine. Neither Nanny nor Granny had enough hairs on their legs to count. As a woman who shaves her legs 365 days a year, the older I get I hope this will be me someday, still hoping.

Nanny quoted this verse uncountable times and ingrained it in our hearts and it has proved to be a family favorite: "And we know that in all things God works for the good of those who love him, who have been called according to his purpose" (Romans 8:28).

Nanny, Pampaw, Nanny's sister Phoebe, and her husband Frank lived in Acton for years, and we frequented their homes. I remember Pampaw snuggled in his recliner, covered in his plaid blanket, watching The Price Is Right. He was a great cook and had many secret recipes which right now I'm wondering if we were ever privileged to. Aunt Phoebe and Uncle Frank attended our church, so we saw them a lot, and he made us the best ice cream cones. We drove from Nanny's to Aunt Phoebe's house on the golf cart, and we thought that was so much fun. We ate fancy dinners at the club looking out over the lake where we fished during the day at the marina, when not swimming.

There was a small store right down the road from our house that had aisles and aisles of penny candy. We used to search the house high and low—couch cushions and all—for change, stuff our pockets full, and head to fill up our brown paper bags as full as we could get them. Handfuls and handfuls we put in our bags, and then we waited eagerly for the cashier to let us know if some had to go back. We certainly hoped that we could keep it all, but occasionally our eyes and desire were more than our change. Even now when I see a brown paper bag, it takes me back to that feeling. No matter how much we were able to bring home, it was enough. What we were given, we were happy with. Life was simple then. What we had wasn't a lot, but it was plenty, and we were happy and satisfied, and we were a family.

❤

Lord, thank You for grandparents and great-grandparents, and their compassion that spilled by the buckets! Sincerely, thank You, Lord, for the memories and that I could recall them (with a little help)! It is my desire, my prayer to become more like them—to give: give love, give time, just give in whatever way that looks like. And when I fail, may Your grace cover me. Lord, may I be a soft rain on a parched soil to someone today.

From my heart to yours:

In all things, I wish you enough.

- Where is your *safe* haven? Where do you find comfort just being there?
- Are you giving of yourself to others, why not start now?

What do you have that you can give someone? (It doesn't have to cost a thing and probably it'll mean more if it doesn't.) Think of the times you've said, "It's the little things." Ponder some of those now. What has He blessed you with? *Is it enough?* Let it be.

My prayer for you:

Lord, show us favor and provide us all a "Granny's house" or a "Mammaw's house," a place where we can step into Your grace and know You are there. Teach us all to be more giving of ourselves—our time, our hearts, and our breaths. Lord, You have given, and You have taken so much from us all over the years. I pray that what we have is enough. You are bigger than anything we have or anything we can imagine. Amaze us, Lord, with simple.

His healing words to your heart:

"Do nothing out of selfish ambition or vain conceit. Rather, in humility, value others above yourselves, not looking to your own interests but each of you to the interests of the others" (Philippians 2:3–4).

Chapter 4:
Living on the Outside Looking In

*Above all, love each other deeply, because love
covers over a multitude of sins. —1 Peter 4:8*

Had our house been made of glass, people would've known
the truth. Walls were built, literally and figuratively, protecting
us, hiding what was within those barriers. Looks sometimes
are misleading, and by this I mean people that "look" really
bad or "different" than us may be wonderful people. After
all, insides aren't seen. Likewise, there are some very beautiful people that are horribly ugly inside. People, who look like
us, or look like society wants them to—clean-shaven and free
of tattoos or piercings—may be horrific people on the inside.
Similarly, "beautiful" people sometimes know they are "beautiful" and are hard to be around. We shouldn't judge by what
we see, though it is easy to do, and I am guilty of this as well.
We all have a certain comfort level that we won't budge from.

In an area not far from where my parents lived, a great

number of people congregated on the street corners with signs asking for money. Most, if not all, of these people appeared to be enslaved by the same addictions that encompassed my mother; though I do not know their stories, hence the previous statement regarding judging people. These people could have just been down on their luck or may have made a variety of bad decisions or choices. We saw this with our parents over and over again! What I did more than anything when I passed them was pray. When I looked at these people, I tried to not judge them or just see an alcoholic, a drug addict; I tried to see a dad, a son, a brother, or someone's mother, someone's daughter, or someone's sister. My heart broke for their stories, for their children's stories. As children of tragic stories, we can't change where we come from, but we can change where we go and who we become.

Our life was a monumental catastrophe most of the time, oftentimes much more than a minor annoyance. I felt as if our family was one tent away from the Big Top. We girls were caught in the middle of the first man we each had ever loved and the woman who wouldn't love us. Lord, thank you for Dadi. We are forever grateful. Where would we be if it wasn't for his love for us? No man could've loved us more.

Children shouldn't be torn between their parents in any situation. No one knows what we concealed under our roof in our fancy house in the Walnut Creek subdivision in Mansfield, Texas. We were the "rich" girls who had "everything"—or so people thought, and all is not what it appears on the outside, as is true for both people and things.

Better a dry crust with peace and quiet than a house full of feasting, with strife. —Proverbs 17:1

Mother provided times that you could "pay for the entire seat, but sit only on the edge." We lived our lives in a calm panic most of the time within a layer of pale-gray film that covered our house from Mother's chain smoking. We girls grew up with True Blue 100's (cigarettes) being a staple when we went to the store. Our house and cars smelled like a stale ashtray, and we definitely weren't the Cleavers. What we really lacked was normalcy and experience—we'd never dealt with an addict before. We were children, so we didn't even know what one was. It was easy for me to comprehend that Mother was an alcoholic, because that was normal. How sad is it that I consider an alcoholic normal? But an addict? I grew up in Sunday school, wearing patent leather shoes, pretty dresses, and bows in my hair. How can I be an addict's daughter?

There were so many moving parts in our lives, but from the outside looking in, I'm sure it looked calm and collected. We had learned to be pros at keeping it together. Truly, I am thankful that God doesn't call the qualified. He qualifies the called. He puts things in our lives that we have no clue how to deal with so we are forced to totally rely on Him, and when we do, we learn valuable things in the lesson. Total dependency, leaning on Him would really come later as when all this really started, I was too young and too immature to understand true dependency and leaning on my Father. Luckily, I had Dadi to lean on and lean into.

Mother was addicted to prescription drugs, vodka, Blue Bell ice cream, and chocolate: M&M'S, Hershey's chocolate syrup, chocolate chips, chocolate icing, and Hershey bars. In all these things, the bigger the better. (Ironically, not long after Mother's death, Blue Bell shut down its production.) I never realized how many different chocolate things Mother was addicted to until I read it in black and white. Initially she hoarded Hershey bars, Hershey's chocolate chips, and vodka, then her commodities became more personal and more precious to her and she began hiding pills. The "crispers" in our refrigerator concealed Mother's chocolate bars and chocolate chips, tucked secretly in the back or under something so we, her children, couldn't find them. Who hides food from their children, even if it's chocolate? When she emptied a can of Hershey's chocolate syrup, she would fill it with milk, stir it, and drink out of it to fulfil her "need" for chocolate, and I can still hear the spoon clanging on the metal can as she stirred. She couldn't stand the thought of some of her "vice" going down the drain or in the trash. The spaces that should've held shoes and sweaters in her closet were lined with vodka bottles that she thought she had hidden from our tiny eyes. Did she not realize little girls go in their mama's closets to play dress up or hang up clothes?

It wasn't until I was older that I really understood that my mother was truly an addict and realized she was addicted to so many things. As an adult looking back, I realize she had an addictive personality. It was easier for me to stay in denial— to think she was just an alcoholic. That seemed "more normal" and more easily acceptable to me, and probably others as well. I remember an entire year that Mother drank chocolate instant breakfast and ate popcorn. These were the two items that sustained her and nourished her body for 365 plus days. These were the only things I ever knew she ate. Who does that? Someone with an addictive personality.

Mother only used Viva paper towels when we were growing up and never, ever, ever went anywhere without a drink. Mother wrapped a paper towel around her red Solo cup (way before they were popular) and secured a rubber band around it, every time without fail. I am realizing now that these "drinks" probably contained vodka. How did I not know then?

They say vodka doesn't smell on your breath, but I will argue this point. Mother's breath had a distinct smell. I remember Mother "smelling" like a drunk, and it was embarrassing. She had so many odd, peculiar behaviors. Remembering the way she was still brings that familiar feeling of confusion. I can remember her close friends saying to me, "Your mom doesn't go anywhere without her drink." I was embarrassed, but didn't really know how to respond, not knowing if they "knew."

Despite the sun shining and pouring through the windows, our house appeared dimly lit. We looked as if we had it all—nice clothes, nice cars, a nice house—but not a home. Our secrets would stay with Mother each year as we packed our satchels and pencil boxes with all our school supplies, and trotted off to school. We looked normal. We looked like your typical family. We harbored so much inside that no one knew; no one suspected the chaos we lived in—just how Mother wanted it (look like the Cleavers but really, you're the Addams Family).

It was at my thirty-year reunion that friends and classmates found out my mom was an alcoholic and addict. My response: "That's why I didn't drink or party in high school." (Truth be known, I probably wouldn't have drunk anyway.) "She was an alcoholic and addict. Y'all just didn't know." Our family had secrets—secrets were burdens, and mothers were very heavy to carry.

Only our closest friends knew something was "odd" with Mother, but still I don't think anyone really "knew" or maybe they did. I was a cheerleader, Miss Mansfield, and Homecoming Queen. I had everything a little girl and teenager would want growing up. Everything but a mother.

❤

Lord, we never really know what You've laid at people's feet, what crosses You've asked us to bear. Definitely, all is not what it appears, so let us see with Your eyes. Thank You for walking with us and I truly pray grace on all the stories left untold. Keep reminding us that Your grace is greatest in our deepest waters.

From my heart to yours:

- Do you judge others by their outside appearance?

- Is what's shown on the outside a true reflection of your inside?

- Have you ever been calm and collected on the outside and falling apart on the inside?

- What "hard" has He given that you had to depend, rely, or totally trust in Him?

- What do you lean into?

- What do you hide from others that only God can see?

My prayer for you:

I pray you will take a breath and trust Him for the next.

His healing words to your heart:

But the Lord said to Samuel, "Do not consider his appearance or his height, for I have rejected him. The Lord does not look at the things people look at. People look at the outward appearance, but the Lord looks at the heart" (1 Samuel 16:7).

Chapter 5:
What I Really Wanted

Cast your cares on the Lord and he will sustain you; he will never let the righteous be shaken. —Psalm 55:22

At first, all I really wanted was a mommy. Little girls need their mommies, every single day, and I was no different. I wanted her to hug me and to hold me closer than a secret; after all, I was keeping hers. As time went by, and adulthood set in, I really just wanted a mother. Right now, I wish I had a mother.

"Even now, after all these years, you, Mother, never wanted the same thing."

"You came first to you."

"You were one of the most selfish people I knew."

"It didn't bother you that you were not there for us, how could it not?"

"How could you sit there in your chair with no emotion?"

"How could you sit and act like we didn't matter, that the missing relationships with your daughters and granddaughters

didn't matter? These things were important, we were important and so were our girls."

"How could your ten minutes a day being awake sustain you?"

"What kind of life is that? You contributed zero to this world, but boy, didn't you take from it."

"What kind of marriage was that for Dadi?"

I can't tell you how many times these questions played over and over in my head, always with no answers.

"Why can't I stop asking them? Why can't I just let it be? Why can't I accept the silence for an answer?"

Desperately, I wanted a mother who loved me and showed me she loved me. I wanted someone who wanted to play with me, shop with me, cook with me, be with me, and laugh with me. I wanted a mom I could grow old with. I pictured myself caring for this older woman who had cared deeply and tirelessly for me. I saw myself combing her gray-tinted hair and helping her walk and stand as her bones had grown feeble and tired. I wanted to return the favor for all she had done for me. I saw our girls helping and caring just the same. I wanted a grandmother for my daughter like I had had. How could she be a grandmother when she had never been a mother? I wanted her to know me.

None of this came to be. In my mind's eye, there was not a woman sipping drinks, tipping pill bottles, passed out in the chair with drool lingering down her chin. This is not the woman I saw in the dreams that I made up of a mother. But, I know it was who He saw. He had a plan and we were helping Him fulfill it, even now our pain is not in vain. "Use me, Lord" has been in so many prayers I have spoken through the years.

Our pain has *purpose.*

It's very funny, comical almost, that I learned so many things not to be from my mother. I learned how to be a mother from her, by not doing what she did. (This is still true today.) I learned how to be something from someone who wasn't what I was learning to be.

How many times had I prayed for a beautiful relationship between Mother and me, a relationship like Ruth and Naomi in the Bible? Ruth demonstrates hesed or loyal love to Naomi that goes beyond the requirements of duty. Hesed means "kindness" or "lovingkindness" and wraps up all the positive attributes of God. It's a quality that moves someone to act for the benefit of someone else without considering "What's in it for me?" I've had a Ruth, and I'm forever grateful that I learned to be one.

Please go read Ruth 1: 8-20. You'll be so *glad* you did.

We girls had the need to be filled with love, not drained of it. Mother drained us and filled us with nothing. We were the children, and we had the need to be mothered. Lacking this caused us to grow up faster than we should, but also helped make us the women we are today. We gather, we love, we share, we give—we, not I. God's grace, nothing but God's grace, facilitated this.

My Dadi adored me, and I was his baby girl. He often called me "tiger." Always a Dadi's girl, and Taylor loves to remind me of that. She's her daddy's girl too, and that's ok as I can never deny the love between a dad and his daughter. Dadi and I laughed together, fished together, went on vacation together, golfed together, played together, wrote together, and worked together. He loved me, and I was head over heels crazy about him! We shared so many breaths together, and I couldn't have loved him more.

He tried to teach me to drive a stick shift, and no amount of skill or talent would be enough to have succeeded that day; however, it is one of the funniest memories I have with Dadi. We laughed; I mean, the kind of laugh that you almost have an accident (not the car accident kind) laugh. I was trying to learn in a Honda Civic, and every time I shifted, Dadi's seat came dislodged and it flung backwards, as in he was flat on his back—all 6'4" of him. We laughed, and he fixed the seat. Then I drove a bit, shifted, and there went his seat again and there he went. We laughed hard. Tears came, but these were happy tears! We laughed so hard that we had to go home as we were hysterical, and all of a sudden learning to drive a stick shift no longer mattered and actually, I never learned how. Life was good that day. We lived that day in spite of anything that was going on back at home. No matter what else was going on in our world, we lived and laughed, and it felt good. We made memories, good memories.

Dadi was Santa and the tooth fairy, he created the best haunted houses at Halloween, and he took us to church. Our Dadi loved us and showed us he did with every breath he took. He tried so hard to make our upside-down world normal even if he wore rose-colored glasses while doing so.

He was handsome, real handsome. All my friends and my sisters' friends thought so, because he was. Dadi had to bend in half to be the height of most. He was tall, and we looked up to him in more ways than just stature. My friends loved him; I didn't know anyone who didn't. I still feel that way. I felt "safe" around Dadi. No matter what went wrong, he was always there for me. He adored me and I knew that; he treasured us all and made sure we always knew this. He did what he could to make our house a home and sweep all Mother's wrongdoings under the rug. He tried, yes, he tried. I would never have wanted to trade places with him as I'm sure his wounds were deeper than ours. He was wounded daily by Mother. I'll never believe that he would have chosen this way of living and never believe that this is what he wanted. Maybe things just got so out of control that he lost his ability to control them, and I'll never fault him for that.

What I wanted was for her to hurt me in a way that would heal (a cut, a bruise, a broken bone). Instead, she shredded my heart into tiny pieces, as if confetti to be thrown in the air. She hurt me until I was broken, and then she kept hurting. She never stopped—just now my pain is numb.

I would never question God's plan for me, for us. I trust Him! How could I not? I did then, and I do now. He knows everything that will happen before it does, and He's not surprised by anything. He goes before me, preparing my path. I find comfort in this, an extreme amount of comfort. I truly trust God with every breath I take. You can't imagine how much faith I have; my faith has sustained me as He keeps covering me with His grace.

Sometimes faith is mandatory. Sometimes things are so out of control and the only choice you have is to have faith and trust Him. We have to truly trust that He is parting waters and moving mountains ahead of us. This will be the moment your life changes by totally trusting Him. One of the greatest compliments David ever gave me was telling me he never knew anyone with greater faith. You can't imagine what this meant to me. I put faith into motion and saw God come through for me. It really wasn't anything I did, but Him working in me and through me. All these breaths later, it is incredibly humbling, overwhelming really when I play back in my head what He did for me. I am forever grateful.

God had so many chances to take Mother, but He let her and us endure her addiction for over forty years! My sisters and I wouldn't be who we are today if we hadn't had these challenges to grow from. We are all teachers and students, learning from our successes, our mistakes, and the mistakes of others. Some day's school is in session longer than normal, and sometimes we never get out for the summer. Sometimes we learn, and sometimes it takes Him teaching and reteaching before we get it.

When I finally do "get it," I often ask myself why I didn't "get it" sooner. I have to tell myself, "He's got this!" Am I really that hardheaded? I will always keep reminding myself that God is in control and we must keep looking for the miracle. In the same Hand that He holds the stars, He holds our hearts, and He holds us.

❤

Lord, thank You for going before me, before us.

From my heart to yours:
- Has God's no ever been your best yes?
- Has there ever been a time in your life when you had to go it alone?

My prayer for you:
I pray that when you see that giant mountain ahead, you will drop to your knees and praise Him that He's already walked ahead. It's frightening and oftentimes paralyzing to trust Him, but let's offer up hallelujahs when we're eye to eye with our giants. When your life changes in a breath into a sad so deep you feel as if you can't make it out, and you feel as if your next breath may be your last, I pray you turn to Him, call on Him, reach for Him, and see Him provide for you. These things I pray.

His healing words to your heart:
"And the child grew and became strong; he was filled with wisdom, and the grace of God was on him" (Luke 2:40).

Chapter 6:

Disappointment
(Failure and Forgiveness)

"Be strong and courageous. Do not be afraid or terrified because of them, for the Lord your God goes with you, he will never leave you nor forsake you." —Deuteronomy 31:6

Sunlight dances on the leaves, but there is safety in the dark. Shadows are a place to hide, and some days I found myself in total darkness. There were many days that I didn't have a mother. She would stay "somewhere" where she was safer, and so was I. Sometimes this meant we were alone in the same house, and other times she was alone in some sort of drug or alcohol rehab. I was way too young to learn what AA was, and I don't even know if they had NA back then. Oh, the silent tears that would flood down my face while lying alone in the bed at night, face buried in my pillow crying, choking down more tears than I swallowed.

Sometimes the pain is so bad that we cry from our gut, and

those definitely were gut tears that would someday heal me. I didn't know if I was more scared for me or for her and who she'd become, but God was always there for me to keep me safe. I know now that He was also there with her, but I wonder if she knew. He kept me in a place that I needed to be—with Him—and this is when I began to learn to trust Him at such an early age. Sometimes we were so fearful, terrified really, and we had no other choice but to trust Him. Nothing else seemed right; this is all we knew.

So many things came and went, and so many things changed during the days she decided she didn't need us or even want us! I wonder when she stopped thinking of me as her little girl. *"When did you decide that your responsibility as a mother was over? This wasn't your choice to make."* When she wasn't there for me, I learned to live without her; I learned to not need her, and this continued my entire life. The older I got, the more hurtful it became for us both. I'm not sure that she hurt like I did, and sometimes I wonder if she even hurt at all, and I saw through a blur of disappointment.

So many years came and went, and she needed me just like I needed her, and my brain was confused; my heart was in a knot. Should I do what she did to me or do the right thing? Who would win the fight, who would give in? I knew who was right, I knew what to do—I needed shelter and she needed forgiveness. I needed love and she needed a witness. Did I have the strength to show her Jesus? Some days I didn't know if I did and some days I knew I didn't. Pure honesty and complete sadness.

So many times, I tried to love "my Dadi's wife" and I couldn't even do that. I needed to show her a four-letter word: love! Sometimes I failed completely because of myself, and sometimes it was completely her fault I failed. One time, when Dadi was released from a stay in the hospital, I went over to take them some food I had cooked. For years, I brought them leftovers as this was a way I could show compassion, and I knew it was a great help to Dadi.

I stopped by the pharmacy to get some medicine for Dadi, and the pharmacy put some medicine in the bag for Mother and I didn't think anything of it. I got to their apartment and began taking the medicine out, and the bottle was Xanax! Are you kidding me! Immediately these words fired out of my mouth: "Mother, are you taking Xanax?"

"Yes," she replied, "And I'm also taking Vicodin and something else! It's my body and I can do with it whatever I want!"

Sad but true. It was her decision. It was always her choice. Why did I keep expecting her to do something different? She didn't change, not then, not ever! Insanity comes to mind. Why did I subject myself to her evil, deliberate doings over and over, thinking she would care? After all, I was trying to be nice and trying to help Dadi by picking up the medicine and keeping him from a trip out while he was recovering. Every time I did something nice and put myself out there, it always backfired—every time!

Well, I heard these words she spoke and I did what I always did: I gathered my stuff and walked out the door. Retreat. It was always safer that way, but once again I hurt Dadi. How many times had we done this same scenario? How many times would I drive myself home trying to see through the tears?

Why did I expect her to change? Some of these memories hurt so badly when I recall them. Believe me, I'm happy that I have memories after everything that's been done to my brain, but still, it hurts. It feels as if I'm there right now. I can hear her voice, her tone and see her hateful expression as she lashed such hateful words at me with intention and not a care in the world. I wish it didn't hurt, but it does. Dadi loved her sober, drunk, or stoned, and I just couldn't.

Clothed in hate, anger, deceit, abandonment, I had to learn to wear the coat of forgiveness. "We are forgiven much, and so we love much, and through the reality of that love, we can extend forgiveness to those who have inflicted some of our deepest pain."[1] This provides peace and comfort every time I read it. I'm able to take a breath, a deep one, and exhale forgiveness while tears drip.

I'm no saint; I've said so many horrible things trying to repay hurt with hurt: "I hate you. I wish you were dead. I wish you weren't my mother." I had to realize that by hurting her I was only hurting myself. Oftentimes pain tumbled from my mouth in the words that I spoke, even before thinking. Through it all I've had to pray that God would soften my edges and bring His grace in the form of a filter. My mouth is one way I know His grace is granted much more than I deserve.

So many storms came, and I voiced so many words that stained hearts and killed joy, and I have caused irreparable damage to ones that I love, for which I am sorry. I know I can never take these words back. Kimberley had to tell me one night, "You can't un-ring a bell," as I had said something to her (whom I adore) that hurt her deeply. We talked it out, and a lot of it was misunderstanding and words misspoken, but I went to bed knowing I had hurt her deeply and I was sorry. I am not perfect, just forgiven and loved unconditionally.

Resurrection is waiting for you. It's His gift.

"Honor your father and your mother, so that you may live long in the land the Lord your God is giving you" (Exodus 20:12). This scripture feels as if it were written just for me. I hear Kimberley's voice over and over in my head telling me

[1] Saskia Wishart, "Forgiven Much, So We Love Much," *She Loves Magazine,* December 13, 2012, http://shelovesmagazine.com/2012/forgiven-much-so-we-love-much.

this is what God wants us to do. This seems so much easier for Kimberley and Courtney. Why is this so hard for me? It is what God wants me to do, and I am totally convicted. I respect Kimberley and the godly woman she is! How could I be His child and not do this? I do not do this perfectly, and some days I do it horribly, but with every breath I'll continue to try.

I am telling you this because it is an area where I truly need your prayers. Pain floods from my soul, and nothing can stop the tears and heal my broken heart. I'm almost hollow inside. I can see her sitting in her recliner: lifeless, careless, hopeless, and unaware of the pain she's caused. During her life, she was never capable of understanding the pain her choices had inflicted on so many due to the destruction she had caused her body and mind. I am just one heart she has broken among so many more. It is devastating to think that your own Mother has broken or shattered her own child's heart. Right now, in every moment, I am called to honor her and I am trying my best.

Love covers–my gaps, my mistakes and the distances between us. —Idelette McVicker, *She Loves Magazine*

You know the old saying that goes, "Unforgiveness is like drinking poison and hoping the other person would die"? I had to come to the intersection of addiction and forgiveness. I had to learn to forgive! And, I did! Forgetting is proving to be the difficult thing for me. So many memories come to the forefront, especially those I want to forget. The difference in her sin and mine is that she continued, and I do my best to move forward without creating more hurt. Mother continued her addiction and all its consequences until the night she rode in the ambulance for the last time. I walked into the hospital that morning knowing she had finally lost her own battle. Her choices and their consequences were severe and eventually those choices took her life, and it's painfully sad.

I know Mother was saved, but oh, was she backslidden. Why wouldn't she come back to Him? Why wouldn't she tell Him she had nothing—nothing to offer? If you have strayed, come back to Him. Nothing is ok when it's all you have! Open palm, open heart.

We are all *forgiven* at the foot of the cross.

Our lives had become like a dance: Mother would take a step forward and I would take a step back. I couldn't step forward as I didn't want to be hurt again.

❤

God, please forgive me where I fail You. Thank You for your forgiveness even in our failures. Lord, I know in Your eyes, Mother's sin was no worse than any sin I've ever committed. Sin is sin. Thank You, Lord, for your conviction on the places we hurt You and on the strength to stop. Lord, may we honor You more than we fail You and may we always be grateful for your mercy and mostly for Your grace.

From my heart to yours:
- Ponder on times you've been let down, or even times you've let others down.
- Who do you need to forgive, or whose forgiveness do you need to receive?

My prayer for you:
Lord, when we *fail* You, show us Your un-failing love. And when we feel abandoned, let us feel Your breath. Show us that

everything You have planned for us is so much greater than anything in our past. I am truly grateful You confirmed this for me! Help us all to forgive and be forgiven.

His healing words to your heart:

"Even now," declares the Lord, "return to me with all your heart, with fasting and weeping and mourning" (Joel 2:12).

Chapter 7:
The Five Silent Years

But You, Lord, are a shield around me, my glory,
the One who lifts my head high. —Psalm 3:3

On and off during my adulthood, Mother and I would go through periods of not speaking. It was easier to slice her out of my life, as being numb felt better than feeling hurt and angry. It was easier for me to act like I didn't have a mother and to just let her live her life without me. That choice stretched out the silence between us. I felt as if we were oil and water, and we probably were. Mother had hurt me deeply, and given the choice between fight or flight, I chose flight.

Dadi and I worked together at Craftmade International, Inc. during the time I found out I was pregnant, and he begged me daily to call Mother and let her know. In a moment of weakness, I did, and as soon as I hung up the phone, I regretted dialing their number. Mother and I hadn't spoken in five years, and it felt as if I was removing a Band-Aid from a wound that had been covered, but had never healed. How often would this scab break back open? Would it ever heal? I remember making the phone call and feeling like I was telling a total stranger something that was so dear and intimate and personal. I knew I was only doing it for Dadi's sake, not mine, and certainly not Mother's. It was moments like this that she was my Dadi's wife and not my mother.

Mother was notorious for acting like nothing had ever happened, and once again she would treat me as if she didn't even know I was hurt, and she certainly didn't see how she had been the one to cause my pain. She answered the phone and spoke to me as if we spoke every day, even though it had been almost 1,825 days since we had. How many times would we continue this same pattern? Why did I feel so much pain and she felt nothing? Why had I left enough space for the knife to slip in?

She always tried to one-up me when I was sick or ailing or when anything had happened, good or bad, that I was trying to tell her about.

I remember lying in the hospital bed prior to having Taylor; I was sicker than I'd ever been. I felt horrible that day, really horrible. I had heard so many beautiful stories of birth and life and I had been told that mine was holding on by a thread. The doctor had just delivered the news that it was likely that Taylor or I would die from HELLP syndrome (hemolysis, elevated liver enzymes, and low platelets), and I lay there thinking, "Mother, to one-up me this time, you're gonna have to die." Our outlook was bleak, and I had no reason to believe that we would live. Horribly painful words had just been spoken to us, and yet my thoughts were on the contest between Mother and me. I desperately needed a mother that day, but that day proved to be no different than any other.

As I write, I can see the room we were in perfectly clear. Due to the severity of my sickness, the insurance company had approved for me to stay for eleven days, but after two I

Shelley Taylor

asked if I could just go home as the possibility was still that I might die, and I knew I would rather die at home than at the hospital. But God had another plan: He saved us—both of us!

I want to share with you what I wrote to Taylor on her eighteenth birthday. It will provide some details about my HELLP syndrome. Perhaps it will give you some insight to how great our God is, how He can do impossible things.

Eighteen years ago, I was sicker than I've ever been, liver and kidneys all shutting down and I was quickly dying. The birth of a child was supposed to be the most beautiful experience and this was quickly turning into a nightmare while awake. I had worked on Friday, feeling so very sick and pain like I had never experienced. I woke up Saturday morning and I knew something was extremely wrong! I was more terrified than I had ever been and lay waiting to deliver you and was told that if I died, delivery would most likely be when it would happen. I asked to stay awake so I would know exactly what was happening to me and you. So many things went through my head and I tried to play out the rest of your life while being drugged to ease the pain and on anti-convulsants to not seize, and the reality of what was happening. ... then, God had another plan! He would intervene and provide His most beautiful blessing in a precious baby girl that I could enjoy for the rest of my life! I couldn't be prouder of who you've become and all your accomplishments. You have made me so very happy and I am so very grateful He allowed ME to be your mom. Thank you, baby girl, for blessing me more than I ever deserve! I love you muches! xo

Why could Mother not just listen with love and compassion or empathy? Why did she feel the need to be better than me? Our lives were not a contest, and if they were, surely, I was losing.

Approximately four years post poisoning and brain injury, Mother would indeed win. The irony that all these years I lived feeling as if my mother was trying to one-up me, and she finally did. She suffered a fall, causing a worse brain injury than mine that would prove to be fatal. Everything about this entire situation made me sick and sad, and finally, the game was over and there were no winners.

Dadi never understood my anger or distance when I was around Mother (mostly for the holidays). I was expected to "welcome" her into my home, and though I tried, mostly I failed miserably. I couldn't comprehend that a holiday, be it Thanksgiving or Christmas, meant I was supposed to put on a smile and have small talk with someone I didn't engage with the other 364 days of the year. It infuriated me that she sat there just letting Dadi wait on her hand and foot with no appreciation whatsoever. I could never, ever deal with her self-ishness.

Waiting on her first great-granddaughter to be born, she sat in her wheelchair passed out in the waiting room. No active participation, no family time. I took a picture of her that day and couldn't look at it without bursting into tears. The proof of her blatant lack of care hurt too much, and I finally deleted it.

One time when Taylor was in preschool, Mother and Dadi drove an hour from Granbury to come visit Taylor, and she barely could get out of the car she was so stoned. I walked to her side of the car, closed the door, and told Dadi to take her home. I cried all the way back into the house. Taylor was distraught, confused at Mother's actions and mine. Yes, I know I was wrong, but I'm just trying to be totally honest with you. It was always hard for me to communicate and interact with Mother, knowing she chose alcohol and drugs over her family. I truly believe that if we lined up a bottle of vodka, a bottle of OxyContin, and me that she would have a hard time choosing me over the liquor and drugs.

Alcohol and drugs are responsible for wrecking cars, families, marriages, and those we love, and there are millions of daughters and sons in America living the legacy that their alcoholic parent left behind. Unfortunately, my sisters and I are three of them, but we push forward, leaning all the while on God to bring us and our children through to the other side.

❤

God, it's me again. I'm so glad I can talk to you about anything. Sometimes I just need to talk, I need to tell someone how I feel and You are always there. You never get tired of hearing me. Thank you for listening. Help me today to honor You in everything I do, everything I see, and especially in everything I say. I love you!

From my heart to yours:
- What choices have you made that affect others? Are you suffering consequences for choices you've made?
- What choices have others made that have affected you?
- Do you choose fight or flight?

My prayer for you:
I pray that your hearts are softened towards those who have hurt you. Lord, I am so thankful that love heals what hate divides. Help us to know that even if we flee, we can't run from Your grace.

His healing words to your heart:
"But You, Lord, are a compassionate and gracious God, slow to anger, abounding in love and faithfulness" (Psalm 86:15).

Chapter 8:
Linked Words and Linked Hearts

For you created my inmost being; you knit me together in my mother's womb. I praise you because I am fearfully and wonderfully made; your works are wonderful, I know that full well. —Psalm 139:13–14

It was within the same year (I'm not for sure of the exact date) that I turned thirty-six that my parents confessed to me that I had been a twin. That night I turned "speechless" into therapeutic writing from just one spoken sentence.

My parents had called to see if I was home and drove an hour to break the news that they had harbored for so many years. I wasn't the youngest of three girls; I was a big sister to a twin brother who was stillborn.

In my wildest dreams or nightmares, I never saw this coming! I collapsed onto the cold black-and-white checkered floor, crying my eyes out. Nothing could have prepared me for those words! My breath came hard, in sync with my pounding chest.

"Why now?"

"Why tonight?"

"Why is this happening?"

"Why me?"

"Why did I live?"

"Why not him?"

"My parents could've had a boy."

"They probably wanted a boy."

These were my initial unspoken thoughts, but the following are the first words I uttered:

"Where is he?"

"Take me to him!"

"I want to see him!"

"I want to go where he is!"

"Why now?"

"Why tonight?"

"Why is this happening?"

"How can you do this to me?"

"Why, why, why?"

My mother answered without hesitation: "We didn't keep him. There's not a body! We threw him in a trash bag. We got rid of him. Back then no one kept stillborn babies."

Wiping tears and snot from my face, I looked at them both while forcefully shaking my head. "Why?" I felt as if I could hyperventilate, overcome with nausea, guilt, and sadness. So much sadness. I looked at Dadi and asked if this was true.

He responded with much brokenness and tears in his eyes, "Yes."

I was beside myself and plead to him, "How could you not tell me? How could you let her do this to me?" I spewed these words: "What else do you have to tell me? Is everything I know a lie? Am I a lie?"

My life had just changed *forever*. I was no longer who I thought I was; I was no longer the youngest of three girls.

Being the baby girl who survived, I felt as if I had kept a son from being born into our family with two daughters. I couldn't now, or in the future, trust what my parents said to me. If they had kept something that important from me for thirty-six years, how could I believe anything they told me ever again? Unfortunately, I never did. If they harbored something this huge, what would keep them from harboring something small? My relationship with both my parents changed dramatically that night and ultimately would never be the same. Our lives changed and our relationships changed, and all of this was completely out of my control. I felt a huge burden had been placed on my back and I was collapsing with each breath I took. I have no recollection of the rest of the night prior to climbing in bed. No memory of words spoken or not, how long my parents stayed, what we did with the food I had been cooking—nothing. I know that so many times it's just been His grace, through my brain injury, that memories have been taken away because if I think of that night, I'm again laced with burden and guilt.

You spoke me into *motion*;
I won't stop until I see Your *face*.

"How would I deal with this information?"
"How do you deal with this information?"
"God thinks I'm stronger than I really am."
"My complete life is a lie. I'm not who I thought I was."
I've always taken what life has thrown at me and made the most of it, and I wouldn't stop now.

I climbed in bed, and words and thoughts quickly filled my head. Laden with guilt, I found a piece of paper and scribbled the word Why? and then slashed through it as soon as it was written. Then, never having written a thing in my life, I wrote the following:

And the Two Became One

What once was two, God made one. What now is pink, once was pink and blue. One small body with a heart as big as two, pink carries on not forgetting the blue.

I spent night upon night researching "twinless twins" and everything "twin" I could find, just trying to understand who I was. I found twinless twins support groups and CLIMBS (Center for Loss in Multiple Births), and I signed me and my mother up. In order to be a member of the twinless twins, the lost twin had to have a name. My parents had never given my brother a name, so I called my mother and together we named him "Benjamin Samuel (Ben)" after my mom's dad, Benjamin, and my dad's dad, Fred Samuel.

This phone call seemed as if it were nothing special to her, as in, we were naming a baby, and it certainly didn't feel as if we were. It was just a phone call to my dad's wife, my Mother, whom I struggled to understand, to name a human that I shared life with twenty-four hours a day for approximately six months. The whole thing seemed surreal or maybe unreal and hurt deeply. I'm not sure Mother ever did anything with CLIMBS; if so, she certainly never mentioned it, but it made me feel as if I was helping to heal her wound even if she didn't care. I couldn't help but wonder then and now if this was the secret that started her addiction.

I knew I had been given this information, at this very time in my life, for a purpose. But would I be strong enough to deal with it and take on the challenge it presented?

God doesn't make mistakes and this was truly my saving grace. He knew I was a twin all along. He knew this information and knew exactly when it would be given to me. He knew how I would react. His grace found me just as I was—nothing more, nothing less. I believe with all my heart that this was His event that put a pencil in my hand so to speak.

She is clothed with strength and dignity; and she laughs without fear of the future. —Proverbs 31:25 NLT

I was overcome with guilt and even over a decade later, I am consumed with the thought "Why me?"

Why Pink?

They say we knew each other, after all you are my brother. I am here and you are gone, why does it all seem so wrong? The things we did, just me and you, until the day our time was through. Did we laugh? Did we cry? Why is it we didn't get to say good-bye? Maybe we did, I don't know, there are so many things left untold. How would you look, how would it be? How is it that now it's just me? Why is it me? Why is it not you? Why did pink win, and not the blue?

On our fortieth birthday, I wrote the following to Ben, to honor him and the breaths I had spent without him:

40 years I've gone without you. 6 months we were side by side. Often it makes me wonder, why you, not me, that died? I want to know what you'd look like. What it would be like if you were here. Going on without you, I never have to wonder if you are near. I'm the lucky one to have had you, if even for such a short time. We carry on together without your body, just mine. Not many can say that they're a twin, and fewer a twinless twin, but no one but me can say they've had a Ben.

*Yet you brought me safely from my mother's womb
and led me to trust you at my mother's breast. I was thrust
into your arms at my birth. You have been my God from
the moment I was born. —Psalm 22:9–10*

Over the years, I have pondered several times, "What if it's not true? What if I wasn't a twin?"

I have no proof other than my mother's word, which lacks integrity on days where my fear is greater than my faith. I know you are probably sitting there thinking, "Why doesn't she just look at her birth certificate?" Believe me, I wish it was that easy, but my Mother had an excuse for everything. It is utterly heartbreaking—almost to the point of a panic attack heartbreaking—for me to think that my parents could drive an hour to tell me a lie. This was a game changer moment. An absolute life changer. If the words they spoke were that— just words—I can't imagine parents doing that to a child. The reality of the sadness remains to this day. I'll never know, and right now, I don't trust or believe anything she ever told me.

This was a time where my life was thread through words. My daughter, Taylor, is dyslexic. Early on in her diagnosis, it was obvious that she wanted to take on the world as she was truly compassionate for those with Dyslexia like her and who struggled with reading. She battled daily with schoolwork and tasks that came so easily for most kids her age, yet a quitter she was not. I knew she had a story to tell, just as I had, learning of my twin. She just wasn't capable of getting her thoughts and words on paper. Could I? Could I do this for her?

I never thought I'd have the courage or strength to write my daughter's story. I could write my feelings, and had done so for quite a while, but could I write someone else's? Someone I was responsible for? Someone that close to me? Would I do her justice or would it be a complete failure for both of us. I have always taken on challenges and pushed myself to the limit, yet would this be a risk I was willing to take? In her few years alive, she had already experienced more failures than I could ever imagine, and I had always been her support, her rock.

God is our refuge and strength,
an ever-present help in trouble. —Psalm 46:1

I spent seven years vigorously researching and writing, following my daughter around with a spiral notebook and sticky notes, truly living my life for Dyslexia. Through her shoes, I saw what she saw, felt what she felt. I was deeply saddened, but also completely overjoyed living and breathing her life. It was ironic to think I had given her life at birth and now she was what was sustaining mine.

We would be the voice of those who could not speak for themselves. My life through writing had meaning and purpose during a time when I felt so meaningless and broken from a troubled marriage. God had given me the ability to write. I was paying it forward and words were mending my heart.

I began by telling her story through my eyes, as her mother, and quickly knew the story had to be told through her eyes to come across to the reader as I had intended. Years went by and finally the last word was written, the ink was set, the tears of accomplishment were dried, and the book was published! My book *Living "Lexi": A Walk in the Life of a Dyslexic* would change lives.

I had what I believed to be an amazing idea as I knew she and I both were so visual. She and I purchased a globe and began putting tacks into it wherever we sold a book. We sent books to Switzerland, Egypt, Australia, Canada, New Zealand, and numerous US states to name a few. This was teaching her that there were children just like her all over the world. Special children, exceptional children with exceptional brains and exceptional lives.

We received emails from people across the world that felt like we had known forever. These people had experienced the same things as my daughter and could totally relate to both her struggles and her victories. Parents were reading her story and feeling as if it was written about their own child. The courage and perseverance that I used to tell her story became her strength in her daily life at home and at school. She has been an inspiration to countless people, dyslexic and nondyslexic alike, and this continues to this day. I never thought I'd learn more from my daughter than what I could ever teach her. This wouldn't prove to be the last time this happened, and I truly could write a book that's entirely a love letter to her alone.

How often have we heard, "One step at a time?" Yet do we really mean it? The size of the step isn't as important as the courage we receive between the steps, which enables us to take the next step, and so on. What gives you that strength? Draw from that, and pretty soon you'll be walking or in my case, writing. If I were to string all my words up as if they were steps, I wonder how far they would reach. Together we've reached across the world. Through this journey, she's reached right into my heart, allowing me to reach so many others. I am forever grateful.

❤

Lord, I am so grateful that You had a plan for my life, just as You do for everyone reading these words You put on my heart.

From my heart to yours:

- I love that I can say the following: God made *me*! He loves me! I was not a mistake! My story is not a mistake! I am here for a reason! I have purpose! I will make a difference while I am here!

- Doesn't it make you feel good just to think these things?

Now, your turn: God made you! He loves you! You were not a mistake! Your story is not a mistake. You are here for a reason! You have *purpose*! You will make a difference while you are here!

- Now write encouragement to yourself, even if it's just *one word.*

My prayer for you:

When their black and white turns to gray, help each reader to still seek You. I pray that each page they turn will encourage them to stay the course, to keep taking the next step, to take their next breath, until they see Your Face.

His healing words to your heart:

"Whether you turn to the right or to the left, your ears will hear a voice behind you, saying, 'This is the way; walk in it'" (Isaiah 30:21).

Chapter 9:
M&M'S for Rehab

Children are a gift from the Lord:
they are a reward from him. —Psalm 127:3 NLT

It was much closer than far; and it was much sooner than later. How many times would we go there? Some version of this moment had happened so many times that we'd lost count. We prayed that this door would never be opened to us again. Same song second verse, over and over and over. Who would be able to endure this longer, us or Mother? Surely another episode would kill our dad.

Rehab again! Mother had passed out at my house, while eating Taylor's birthday cake. Yes, her head just dropped right into the piece of cake on her plate in front of not only us but our friends and Taylor's friends. We were all extremely embarrassed and covered in both anger and sadness. I might mention that this happened just shortly after she had placed half of a hot dog in her mouth, and she passed out while swallowing, causing an enormous choking episode. This was indeed a birthday to remember, unfortunately for all the wrong reasons.

This same scenario had repeated itself time and time again while sitting in her recliner; she would pass out in mid conversation and at the most inappropriate times. Because of her many blackout episodes, she doesn't remember the pain she has caused. She doesn't recollect our hurt, our embarrassment, our shame. She woke every day to a new day, yesterday's words and events are not remembered. Our most painful memories are just that—ours.

Another trip to Granbury, not for fun! Courtney and I met at Mother and Dadi's, walked in the front door, and told Mother as we entered, "Go get packed, you're going to rehab!" I know her heart must've been pounding with both anger and fear as she and Dadi were taken totally off guard (and angry with Courtney and me as well as fearful of the approaching days without her drugs).

"How is it that you are so 'not' a mother that your children can walk in and take control of you and your life? Why are your children the adults?" Boy, did we have to grow up fast. We made grown-up decisions much, much sooner than most.

Well, Mother went to pack all right and came out with a bag that consisted of nothing more than panties with burnt holes in them and M&M'S!

"Are you kidding me? That's what you are taking—M&M'S?" I asked.

She definitely had an addict brain and personality. Who does that? Who only needs M&M'S? I can still recall being both angry, sad, and mortified that this was our life. None of this felt real.

I often wondered if Mother ever thought of us while in rehab; after all, she couldn't medicate her thoughts or her memories. She was faced with reality! When not in rehab,

Mother was either passed out, or when she was awake, unlike us, she never climbed in bed like normal and listened to the sounds of the house—she just passed out. I wonder where her mind wandered while she lay in the bed all those times in rehab, hoping it went to us, but the likelihood of that happening was small to none.

While in rehab, Mother said exactly what the doctors and psychiatrists wanted to hear. She was the valedictorian and a certified manipulator. She said exactly what she thought we wanted to hear. We had heard it before and knew not to trust her, even when she was so convincing. These were some of the times that I hated what she did to our hearts. These were the times when I wanted to believe her words; she was my Mother—how could she lie to me? These were the times when you could tell what workers have great experience with addicts and which ones are "green" so to speak. The ones that were "green" looked at you like you were uncaring, uncompassionate, and the ones with experience knew why you reacted like you do. It was always sad to see the families that were "new" to this as we once were them, and we knew what they had to look forward to and the heartache that was ahead. "She would never touch the drugs again. She would never hurt us again. She was sorry!"

Really? No, she was not sorry! To this day, she was not sorry. She died not sorry. She did touch the drugs again and she did hurt us, over and over again! Years have passed since those days, and if she were alive now, she would be at their apartment swallowing pills. Pills that in her mind would have sustained her; pills that she thought would give her one more breath, one more second, one more minute, one more hour, one more day, one more escape from reality.

Mother did nothing with the *breaths* she had been given.

I can see myself sitting next to her in an uncomfortable metal chair with even more uncomfortable words being spoken in a group counseling room. I can hear her speak lies to us, her children. Her children? Every Mother's Day is hard!

God was daily investing breaths and heartbeats in her, and she just sat and sat, and slept and slept, in her recliner until time for bed. She woke and did it all again. Days went by, months went by, and years—our lives passed her by.

Checking Mother in at rehab (actually, we were in the psych ward of a hospital in downtown Fort Worth), they stripped her naked and looked her over for bruises, etc. She stood there in front of me with aged skin covering her bones. Some places it was just hanging on, and it was sickening to look at her frame and stature and know it was a true picture of the destruction she had done.

They made notes in her chart of her preexisting wounds, which were many. I felt as if they should check me for bruises. Doesn't someone want to take note of how I feel, or my wounds? Mine were on the inside, covered for no one to notice. My heart was broken, but I appeared fine, especially when people were watching.

Mother, on the other hand, had bruises on the outside from a recent incident. She had accidentally set herself on fire while smoking with oxygen in her nose. I know what you are thinking: "What!" I know, so were we. Every time I tell this story, I am shocked and appalled thinking that my mom did this. It is almost incomprehensible to most people, myself included. Mother not only caught her shirt and shorts on fire, but she seriously burned her legs as the flame skipped down them. Luckily, due to what she had previously ingested, she probably felt no pain. This was the one time that being an addict did her some good. Fire went down the hose, burning everything it touched.

Dadi, scared to death, had to stomp out the fire on the

carpet, with his feeble frame, before the oxygen tank that helped sustain her exploded and the house engulfed in flames. Meanwhile his wife, expressionless, surely not panicked in her flame-drizzled clothing, sat there while he did all the work. This was common for her to do things such as this, and Dadi would have to pick up the pieces. Mother left him in the trenches, taking shrapnel for her every day.

The picture in my head of my feeble father stomping out this fire, trying to save both of their lives, makes my heart sicken. Yet another selfish act on our mother's part; there seems to be a pattern here. How much could Dadi endure? How much could he take? Mother and Dadi lived things daily that most people could never comprehend or fathom and would most certainly never face in a lifetime.

Here I was, a grown adult, still pondering, as so many times before:

"When did you stop thinking of me as your little girl who needed her mommy? Why did you not want me? What gave you the right to 'bail' on motherhood? We were on a journey together—you, Dadi, my sisters, and I—one foot in front of the other, and you got off the path; you stopped walking. You released the grip you had on our hands, yet we kept walking; we continued walking without you! We would never know how it felt to finish the race with a mother by our side."

Jesus walked with me, *every step* of the way.

"What will you say when you look into His Face?"

This was a great question for her, but likewise it's a great question for all of us. One day we will all have finished our race on earth and we will look into the face of Jesus.

He entrusted us to her. You don't get to just say, "I'm done mothering." It's a lifelong commitment. If you're a mom and you're reading this, "I'm so proud of you!" Some days, a lot of days, most days, it's the hardest job ever. There's no rule book, playbook that could ever prepare you for little ones. Making them is the easy part—that takes little time, little investment. Then … well, you know! Nothing prepares you.

❤

Lord, nothing could've prepared me for Mother's actions this time around. Another drive to rehab. Thank You for riding with us once again.

From my heart to yours:
- Have you ever had to make "grown-up" decisions before you were ready?
- Are your priorities in the right places, or do you pack M&M'S?
- When your race is done, will you have made Him proud?
- How can you be a better parent, grandparent, or caregiver? Think of something simple and begin today.

My prayer for you:
When things happen along your journey that are totally unbelievable, *believe in Him*. Believe that no matter what He lays at your feet, He is still pursuing you. I pray He teaches us to live our breaths without regret.

His healing words to your heart:
"Trust in the Lord forever, for the Lord, the Lord himself, is the Rock eternal" (Isaiah 26:4).

Chapter 10:

Giving Her to Jesus

He sent out his word and healed them;
he rescued them from the grave. —Psalm 107:20

When I had finally had enough of Mother's shenanigans, the tension was more than I could bear, I called to tell her I wanted a divorce; I no longer wanted her to be my mother. I told her I couldn't take the stress of our broken relationship, and I never wanted to speak to her again. I expressed that to act like she didn't exist was the only way I could survive and lessen the pain. Yes, I know this was wrong, but sometimes we go to drastic measures, and yes, this shattered my already broken heart. While I don't remember her exact reply, I remember she just answered very matter-of-factly with some sort of ok, as if I had called to say, "Be there shortly." The entire conversation took less than two minutes.

A week later, my phone rang and I could see it was Dadi, and by the sound of his voice, I could tell he was scared to death! He was pleading with every stressed breath for me to come help him. I could tell by his voice that something wasn't just "wrong," but that a chain of events had occurred that we could never stop. I was in my truck within minutes to come to his aid. I can vaguely see myself out back watering the flowers, but I have no idea what I did with Taylor or anything of that nature; I just know I left, quickly, without hesitation, to drive an hour to his rescue.

Time is your ally before a crisis, and your enemy during. So many things ran through my head during the hour drive to Granbury, so many scenarios, so many what ifs. I didn't know if I should be angry or sad. I just knew I was both. I was truly about as mad as I could be and as sad as I'd ever been, all balled up into one. Was this the end ... again? I was terrified for Dadi, so sad for him and his love for Mother, and my gut was wrenching while I tried to focus on driving and seeing through the tears. God had invested countless breaths into Mother and they never seemed enough. My heart ached for what He continued doing for her and her lack of care. It was a gift she took but never said thank you for.

Courtney had taken Mother to the doctor earlier that day and had stopped to get Mother dinner, then she left her watching TV and eating her sandwich. When Courtney left, Mother was fine. Dadi later walked into the house to see a woman possibly taking her last breaths, and that woman was his wife and soul mate—that woman was our Mother. In desperation, Dadi called an ambulance that arrived shortly afterwards, and the first responders immediately intubated her.

She was seizing, and later the bruises told us exactly where her body had flailed into whatever was in its path. When I arrived at the hospital, after an hour's time had passed, her hands and face were morbidly swollen, she was almost unrecognizable, her temperature was 105, she was septic, her white blood count was over nineteen thousand, and her blood sugar was over five hundred. What's more, she had COPD and was on a ventilator, and they had restrained her while they waited the results of a CT scan.

Her entire trauma room was filled almost to capacity with doctors, nurses, and therapists. I can remember thinking that all these people were trying to save someone who wouldn't even save herself. They were trained to save lives, and that was exactly what they were doing. Because this was a smaller hospital and this type of patient isn't there frequently, you could see pure terror on some of their faces and a look of normalcy on ours. Here we would go again: adrenalin kicks in and our hearts would stand guarded. We paced with a fair amount of frustration, confusion, and pure disbelief.

Almost immediately upon my arrival, they told us that she was much too serious for their hospital and they were going to airlift her to Fort Worth. I stood outside arm in arm with Dadi as they lifted her off. I even took a picture of the helicopter as it rose in the air as it was a very surreal moment, not knowing if she would live or die. I sincerely prayed God would take her as this was not any form of living.

That night as they took her away in the helicopter, from Granbury to Fort Worth, it was if that's when she left us forever, never to be the same again. She would never truly know us again, and we would not know her. The mom we had known was not the mom that was with us now, and unfortunately, she certainly wasn't the mom that birthed us. Drugs and alcohol had certainly taken its toll on her body, and unfortunately it was taking a toll on Dadi's and ours the same. Our lives would be forever changed and my heart would be forever empty in the space that was meant for her. We began living and breathing with hesitation, not knowing what would present itself here on out.

God allows things to happen that we have absolutely *no control* over, and this was one of those times.

Dadi rode with me in my truck, and few words were spoken. Silence was somehow the key to self-preservation. It was if the silence demanded the obvious conclusion—Mother had yet again disrupted our family—and my heart ached deeply for Dadi.

We arrived at Harris Methodist in downtown Fort Worth, yet again not knowing what to expect. How could her brain continue to survive with all the misuse it was given over the years? How could she keep surviving when we barely were? Mother wasn't conscious, so I didn't know if she knew we were there or not, nor if she could feel our pain.

Mother's seizure activity was so severe that they had to put her in a phenobarbital coma to relax her brain, and for 24 hours she couldn't be disturbed. She lay there in a red cap with electrodes surrounding her head, covering countless amounts of destruction from years and years of abuse. "Was this the end?" we kept asking ourselves. They basically turned her brain off, similar to shutting down a computer, and some things came back and some did not—ok, a lot did not.

Mother stayed in neuro intensive care for one month—one month that totally changed our lives forever! We almost lived at the hospital, Dadi especially. Dadi wouldn't leave her side. Sometimes we stood by her bed, holding our breath, wondering if and how she could maintain hers. Dadi prayed and prayed. We prayed and prayed. The prayers I prayed and the prayers Dadi prayed were different. My Dadi almost offered his soul to save her. He promised to always take care of her if God would save her just one more time.

One more time.

And Dadi kept this promise until years later when she took

her final breath. I remember telling God to just take her. I was tired of hurting, and I couldn't do this anymore. My strength was failing and on some days, it was gone. I would never have the chance to have a mother like I wanted. I knew as long as she was on this earth, I still had a slight chance, no matter how small to have the mother I had always dreamed of.

We met many wonderful families during that month together. We heard stories of tragedy, loss, and love and linked hands and hearts for each other's families. We pled to God for healing and peace, knowing sometimes hearts are healed even when bodies are not. Dadi grew older during that month, weaker and more fragile, while his love for Mother grew stronger. He was faithful. The most faithful any man could be for his wife. Dadi knew the love a husband should have for his wife, and he showed her and us that love, and this would prove to be the love we wanted and desired from our husbands.

One night after leaving the hospital, thinking that her breath and heart would not be able to continue, I wrote these words.

Beside this empty bed, God never leaves her side. Why was it within herself she always had to hide? I hope there's no pharmacy in heaven, she'll find it if it's there. No pills in heaven will she want will always be my prayer. The next time I see her, she will be free. Free from the drugs, free from the need. They're a powerful thing, these drugs that we sell, they can strengthen your body or put you through hell. My prayer is that no one else will go through this pain, so Mother's death will not be in vain. No one could put a number on the years that she just slept, not knowing we were there, not knowing we wept. Change for us ... for our children ... for yourself ... we pled. She never listened, and now she is Dead.

The next morning:

Wait … God chose not to take her, with us she would stay, leaving us all, in total dismay. Would she pay for her choices, was suffering in store? Will she feel the agony she caused us, and more? There are so many things, I'll never understand, but one things for sure, God sticks to His plan. Question Him not, He'll show us in time. Have faith in Him, and He'll calm our minds.

I wrote this another night, wanting so badly to let her know we were here for her, if only she wanted us. She didn't!

What would she choose? It seemed as if her whole life was hanging on by a thread … her family waiting to see if she would come back to us or if the scissors would cut the only thing left that was holding us together—this would be told by the decision she would make … she couldn't understand that even though the once beautiful quilt had been torn, ripped, and in some areas shredded, we were waiting for her with needles and thread if given the chance … she was as though the pin cushion and we were all the pins drawn to her side … she had become the thimble— callused, hard, and as if stonelike to protect the inside that was so delicate … we were waiting to take the small steps to reach our goal of having her back … please let us mend you, for you can't do it alone.

My heart will always have aches and pains for what will never be. That person left many years ago when she started her abuse, never to return. After that hospital stay, even if she wanted to be that person, she was physically and mentally incapable of doing so. Her destruction was severe, both to her and to us. Mother didn't even know how to use a cell phone. Dadi had a flip phone that he kept with him, and he bought Mother an even simpler one to keep while he was gone in case of an emergency. We tried numerous times to teach her how to dial 911, and she just couldn't do it.

Even after she recovered and came home, the episodes of drama would never stop. Dadi collapsed in the floor with an abdominal aneurysm, and Mother didn't know how to call 911 and had to go downstairs, maneuvering her good leg, to their neighbor's apartment and summon her help. Mother had to knock or beat on the door loud enough to wake the neighbor with her nondominant hand as her good hand was paralyzed from prior strokes. This took quite a while for her to get down the stairs with one leg paralyzed; meanwhile, Dadi lay there close to death with his stomach filling with blood to the point that it looked like it was going to explode upon our first sight of him. Dadi's life was depending on someone who couldn't even depend on herself.

A couple of days later, Taylor was delivering food to Mother that we had made, and upon her arrival, Mother was at the downstairs neighbor's apartment asking for pain pills, for her, not Dadi. You know, because when your husband is laid up in the hospital after almost dying is when you should make a drug deal, right? It was always about her, even in the middle of someone else's life-and-death situation.

Mother's mind and brain were severely damaged and would never be the same, and it is my hope that this damage is what would cause her to make these kinds of choices. Mother's capability of knowing reality just wasn't there, yet she still had the ability of knowing how and where to retrieve pills for her addiction.

We *love* the sinner, not the sin.

The definition of *endeared* is to "cause to be loved or liked." She was our Mother, and we were endeared to her because of who she was, because she was our Mother. We loved her because of who she was, not because of what she was. I loved her out of responsibility mostly as I never really felt loved by her. She would lean on a walker for strength, and we would lean on Him.

❤

Lord, sometimes You call us out onto the water,
where we just can't hold on any longer,
and we have to give it to You. It's breathtaking and
incomprehensible, the lavishness of Your grace.

From my heart to yours:

- What is something or someone you had to give over to Jesus?

- Have you ever thought there was an end and you got a *second chance*?

- Have you ever made a promise that's been hard to keep?

My prayer for you:

May the Lord give you faith: "confidence in what we hope for and assurance about what we do not see" (Hebrews 11:1). May He send it extravagantly to you and may you believe when it makes no sense at all. My prayer is that's when His grace will follow.

His healing words to your heart:

"In him we have redemption through his blood, the forgiveness of sins, in accordance with the riches of God's grace" (Ephesians 1:7).

Chapter 11:

What Fills the Cracks
in our Broken Hearts

However, I consider my life worth nothing to me;
my only aim is to finish the race and complete the
task the Lord Jesus has given me—the task of testifying
to the good news of God's grace. —Acts 20:24

God's grace, His sweet, sweet grace! My sisters and I have often said that God "poured His grace right over our heads," filling in all our cracks, while drowning us in His mercy. His grace covered us, and mercy sent the hurt and pain away. He breathed new life into our souls, so we could one day pay it forward. *The grace of God is glue for the broken and sometimes our broken is shattered.* Let Him breathe in you a new life.

But be sure to fear the Lord and serve him faithfully
with all your heart; consider what great things
he has done for you. —1 Samuel 12:24

Over and over I think of how God has poured His grace on our family, on us girls, on Dadi. But right now, I can't help but think how He poured His grace on our mother. He helped her carry on. He was the reason she was alive, if only she knew this. She didn't think of Him. Her thoughts were far from where He was. He had so many chances to take her and He chose to sustain her—while sustaining us! God's second chances seem to never run out. We are bound to be heavy by now. His inexhaustible grace had been hers, freely given and taken without her even realizing it. It's because of Him that we can stand! God had mercy on our mother. God's grace is beyond my comprehension!

> *Grace is free sovereign favor to the ill-deserving.*
> *—Benjamin B. Warfield*

(Myself included!)

> *That is the mystery of grace: it never comes too late.*
> *—Francois Mauriac (1885–1970)*

(His timing is impeccable.)

No matter what you've done, He's waiting. You're never too old or never too bad for His second chance. Sin is sin to Him, and all sin is the same. In His eyes, one white lie is no different than the worst sin you can imagine, the one in your thoughts right now. He loves you. Love won on the cross. That stands repeating: Love won on the cross!

> *"Though your sins are like scarlet,*
> *they shall be as white as snow." —Isaiah 1:18*

God's grace is unending and available for everyone, even you—*especially* you!

❤

Lord, thank You for Your grace! Thank You for pouring grace on us when we least deserve it. Lord help us to truly grasp that grace is free and we are forgiven in You. May we extend grace to others, especially those we deem undeserving. May we be more like You I pray.

From my heart to yours:

- How has *God* extended you grace?

- How have *others* extended you grace?

- Who can *you* extend grace to?

My prayer for you:

I pray He pours grace right over your head and breathes in you a renewed sense of life. It is appointed to everyone to die, but not everyone lives while they're here. I pray you live. Grace normally comes when we least expect it, when we think we are undeserving, when we're full but feel empty. That's the beauty of grace.

His healing words to your heart:

"Praise the Lord, my soul; all my inmost being, praise his holy name. Praise the Lord, my soul, and forget not all His benefits—who forgives all your sins and heals all your diseases, who redeems your life from the pit and crowns you with love and compassion" (Psalm 103:2–4).

Chapter 12:

Embracing

Cherish her, and she will exalt you; embrace her,
and she will honor you. —Proverbs 4:8

I believe in embracing the small and the big moments, the beautiful and the broken. I believe in hugs—tight, long hugs. I believe in a mother's skin-to-skin, heart-to-heart bonding with her children. Actually, I believe we should all hug heart to heart, no matter what age, what an amazing feeling blending hearts. People should be held tight, not at arm's length. Trey and Ross Taylor (my two sons) both do this exceptionally well, and greet me with a hug every time they see me!

I can't remember Mother hugging us as children. I can't remember her embrace. As an adult, when I hugged Mother, it was awkward, stiff, uncomfortable, and empty, resembling my relationship with her. It was only done out of obligation. "Did she bond with us? Was there not a place in her heart where we girls once belonged? Did it not feel empty now that we were not there?"

There were so many years that I felt so empty, and friends and family received empty hugs from me. I didn't feel worthy of receiving love from others because I had been told I wasn't good enough by the one who mattered the most to me. Compliments and touch didn't exist in our home. While I wanted love and affection so badly, I was in a place where I couldn't receive it from my family because I had been hurt so deeply. I longed to be wholly embraced. I wanted this so badly but guarded my heart from receiving it from others as I was torn, not knowing if I deserved it or not. The latter won.

I believe in kissing—sweet, soft kisses or sloppy, long kisses. Just the connection of the lips, just like the connection of the embrace. Just kiss; it's important, no matter how young or how old you get. I love that my grandbabies, my "littles" love to pucker. I can remember Dadi kissing me on the forehead when I was young, I think because he was so tall he bent until he reached skin, but the touch was amazing, sweet, and special. And speaking of, I love to stand on my toes and kiss! I love that David is tall as this is "love squared" for me. I love blowing kisses and giving and receiving Eskimo and butterfly kisses. Again, kissing is important: whether on the cheeks, lips, or hands—just kiss! Give and receive; it'll make a difference to you, the giver, and especially the receiver.

No matter how big or how small, leave *love*.

Our Dadi loved to hug; he was the greatest hugger! My Dadi hugged everyone he came in contact with, with the most incredibly tender embrace. Strangers were not strangers long after his gentle, frail body engulfed them. Sitting at our Dadi's dying bedside, we spoke of Dadi's hugs and how we will miss them. No one hugged like Dadi. You were engulfed in both of his arms that reached entirely around your body and felt nothing less than a feeling of love and safety.

This made me think of the story I wrote years ago when Dadi had to quit work to provide Mother with full-time care. Dadi was a custodian at Baccus Elementary, where he loved many and was loved by many.

Good-bye, Mr. Bill

Life had changed for Mr. Bill at 5741 Flint Drive. His deeply lined face showed the years of stress that had taken a toll on him. Soon he found that what seemed so important, before coming to Baccus Elementary, wasn't so important anymore.

Mr. Bill had been a great provider for his family and his children couldn't have asked for more. How could the jobs that he had before ever compare to what he had now? He found himself at an elementary school where money proved not near as important as the countless hugs that he would receive.

It was said that he had been given over 300,000 hugs in the 6 years he was there. He was a man of grand stature, yet reachable by all. He was not only the head custodian, but a sincere listener and father to many. He was a father to those still celebrating single-digit birthdays and those who had taught at Baccus more years than the students had been alive. Mr. Bill was truly loved by all who knew him and by those who had only knew of him.

Every holiday or special event brought artwork he had created, and little pieces of him soon filled the school with excitement. The children looked up to him, and he loved them all, no matter what color, what size, or what intelligence level. Baccus had truly become his home. Yes, he had come to be the custodian but had settled in as part of their family. Out of all the places he had worked, he was finally somewhere where they needed him as much as he needed them.

Mr. Bill put great pride in all the work he did at Baccus, and it truly showed. The faucets in the school shined so much that you could see your reflection. And just like the faucets, this was a true reflection of who he was. He had a wife, three daughters, and five granddaughters who loved him as well. When some of his granddaughters moved five hours away, the children at Baccus helped him to still feel connected with them.

Mr. Bill had a huge heart and it became ill at times. He would have bouts of hospital stays and would be missed upon not entering the school in the mornings. Baccus wasn't Baccus without Mr. Bill. His caring ways brought many tears to those at Baccus. He impacted not only the staff, the students, but their parents as well. After the death of one of the students, he was asked to speak at their funeral. What an enormous honor for a custodian.

Mr. Bill's wife had been sick for many years and he had always known that the day would come when he would have to leave his family at Baccus and care for his first love back on Flint Drive. This decision was made after countless prayers and many, many tears. After not showing up for days, some of the students asked if he had passed away.

Everyone agreed that there needed to be a special way to say good-bye to Mr. Bill and let him know how much he was loved. One could not let him leave without bestowing on him some of the love and compassion that he had provided to so many each and every day. It was decided,

Baccus would have "Mr. Bill Day"! Family members surprised him from out of town to help celebrate his special day. "Mr. Bill! Mr. Bill!" chanted throughout the cafeteria by every student and staff member to get things under way. He was honored with boxes of letters from students and staff, countless hugs and an enormous amount of tears. Students signed T-shirts for him so no one would ever be forgotten. He had received many awards and recognition throughout his tenure at Baccus, but nothing could compare to this special day.

Mr. Bill is at home now, taking care of his wife, and will be missed by all. Who would have known that a custodian could make such a difference in so many lives? With gentleness, he kneels beside his bed and thanks God for the memories that will forever be embedded in his heart. And he remembers the children's cries, "Good-bye Mr. Bill!"

> *In his Hand is the life of every creature*
> *and the breath of all mankind. —Job 12:10*

Touching is important, holding hands, touching hands and hearts. Sometimes we just need to press into each other. We need people. Show those you love that you love them. It'll make a difference to not only you but them, I promise.

We all never really know the things that we will do that will make a difference to others. Some small thing to you may be big to someone else. During some horribly broken years, Courtney handwrote very special letters to Taylor and me that changed our world. On days when I know her hands were too weak to pen, due to her Parkinson's, she still did. She may never truly know what she meant and still means to us. Just to know she cared enough to sit and pen from her heart and link words regarding things that mattered not only to us but to her made a huge difference. Taking on our pain while physically battling her own, she celebrated who we were, and she encouraged us to take that next breath. She was there for us. Possibly you could offer someone a gentle smile, and it would cost you nothing. This one small thing you do may be a miracle that someone has been waiting on. We can make a difference. If we all made a difference to just one person, the outcome could be huge. You may be one breath from changing the world.

❤

Lord, pull me in close today where I can feel
Your breath, and teach me to spill joy,
teach me to drip Your light, teach me to shine.

From my heart to yours:

- What do you embrace, what is dear to you?

- Who can you embrace better? (Maybe just begin with yourself.)

- What is something you can do for someone else? Think of that person who has made a difference in your life and try to be like them, if only for today. *It's a beginning.*

My prayer for you:

Lord, thank You for embracing us. Thank You for pulling us in close when we feel alone and for sending us people to embrace us when we feel unlovable and unworthy. Help us all to seek those who need You, those who need comforting. Help us to engulf them with Your love.

His healing words to your heart:

"Love and faithfulness meet together; righteousness and peace kiss each other" (Psalm 85:10).

Chapter 13:

Unconditional Love

Love bears all things, believes all things, hopes all things,
endures all things. —1 Corinthians 13:7 ESV

Dadi, with his deeply lined face, would never leave Mother's side, literally and figuratively! Through all these years, as frail as he got, he always stood up for her. Her real knight in shining armor. The years took a toll on him—the stress, the sadness, the waiting on her hand and foot. There were so many times near the end when he was at the hospital with her as she had taken yet another fall or was sick again. He was always by her side, barely standing, but standing just the same. He always promised he would eat before heading for home, but I would know by his voice that he was weak and weary. After everything he had supported her through, not much on this earth sustained him. He would never be satisfied unless he cared for her himself as no one could do it as well as he wished.

How many more times could she fall?

How many more times could he keep standing?

We learned so much about commitment and Christ's love by watching Dadi and his relationship with Mother through the years. If we learned nothing else from all we went through, we learned that a husband can truly love his wife as Christ loved the church. Dadi loved Mother that way. It would create an image of a husband that us girls would never forget. Dadi portrayed Christ's unconditional love over and over out in front of us while we watched. David has commented multiple times about Dadi's love for Mother.

For God so loved the world that he gave his one and only Son, that whoever believes in him shall not perish but have everlasting life. —John 3:16

As small and frail as Mother had become, Dadi was too weak to lift her. Dadi made a pallet on the bedroom floor for her as he could not get her back in the bed after she fell. Why couldn't he see that she didn't need to be at home with him? It wasn't safe, not for him or her. His skin was so thin you could see through it. It seemed as though Band-Aids held him together.

My Dadi made a promise to God that he would care for her all the days of his life. Our dad was the epitome of unconditional love, and his life would be shortened because of this promise. He gave our Mother his all, which at times was not much, but it was all he had. For us as we watched, we would know, it was enough. My Dadi would take his last breath declaring her rights. I know he had such a hard decision to make, choosing her over us, but now, after all these years, I get it. I hope Dadi is rewarded greatly in heaven for the love he showed her. I'm thankful they will spend eternity in each other's arms in the presence of the Almighty.

And I pray that you, being rooted and established in love, may

have power, together with all the Lord's holy people,
to grasp how wide and long and high and deep is the love of
Christ, and to know this love that surpasses knowledge—
that you may be filled to the measure of all the fullness of God.
—Ephesians 3:17–19

❤

Lord, I know how much my Dadi loved Mother!
I know so many times I broke his heart, which, in turn,
broke Yours. Thank You for Dadi's love for her. Thank You that
our Dadi set the bar so high and showed us what it means to
love deeply. This is the kind of love I always wanted. I wanted
someone to love me like my Dadi loved my mother, and You
provided that. Truly, Lord, thank you for David.
That bears repeating: thank You for David!

From my heart to yours:
- Who knows the real you and loves you just the same?
- Who do you extend unconditional love to?

My prayer for you:
My prayer is that He provides you someone who shows you unconditional love! My Dadi was God's grace in physical form to my Mother, just as David is to me, and there were so many times I felt I was undeserving. I pray when you turn the last page that you will know, without a shadow of a doubt, that you are deserving. I pray we all begin extending His unconditional love to others, myself included.

His healing words to your heart:
"But God demonstrates his own love for us in this: While we were still sinners, Christ died for us" (Romans 5:8).

Chapter 14:
Striking the Match
(Mother's Epic Fail)

You let people ride over our heads;
we went through fire and water, but you brought
us to a place of abundance. —Psalm 66:12

Burn, baby, burn! This is the day we would find out just how much we could all take. It was a day when the obscene became the acceptable. We were filled with disbelief, horror, and great amounts of sadness. It was a day that our family would never truly forget; it would change our lives forever. Our lives had been transformed through the years from Mother's actions, but never like this, never to this degree! Our lives were altered, deeply; our lives were changed by ashes! It was a day when I wished the blood that ran through my veins was not the same that ran through my Mother's. It was a day, a beginning where we knew …

Only God could bring beauty from the ashes.

Our mother intentionally set their house on fire. Mother's actions took our breath away—they left us speechless. But this was a time when we knew we couldn't remain silent. I penned these words for the fire marshal after we called and turned our mother in for arson. These are some of the saddest words I've ever written, and some of the saddest words I've ever read. I was in total disbelief as to how she could have ever thought this was the right thing to do. This was an event that showed me she wasn't mentally sound in any form or fashion. This is one chapter that is so difficult to put in print, but it showcases addiction in its truest state.

I can't help but think that once again Mother one-upped me. She set the fire in April, just two months after Taylor and I had been poisoned, almost fatally, by carbon monoxide. Attention had been drawn to Taylor and me due to the severity of our brain injuries, and Mother once again had to turn the focus off us and back on her.

Sometimes life is just not fun, and this was one of those times.

I was at work on the phone with my eldest sister, Kimberley, when she told me that Courtney (middle sister) was calling on the other line. Kimberley put me on hold while she answered Courtney, then immediately came back and frantically said, "Let her talk to Courtney," because she was at our parents' house and there was an emergency. She initially told me that Mother had put a cigarette on the carpet and started a fire. I spoke with Courtney, who told me the same about the cigarette. I could tell it was a crisis, and I told Courtney that I would leave work and be there ASAP.

When I arrived, everyone was outside and Mother was sitting on her walker under the carport. I asked Dadi if I could go inside, so he came with me. I grabbed Dadi's cheeks upon entering, just inside the living room, and asked him in a quivering voice, "Don't you know that something is wrong with Mother? She is not right mentally to have done this." He said yes. He was very emotional as were all of us.

I don't remember how Mother came to be on the front porch—maybe when I was inside Courtney helped her—but when I came out the front door, Mother was sitting on her walker just outside. I was confused. I drilled Mother as to why she would do this and how she did it. She proudly told me that she put a cloth in the trashcan and lit it with her lighter. Her plan was to have the house burn down, literally she said "explode" from the oxygen tank.

I asked her at one point did she remember that the oxygen tank was in there and she said, "Yes, that's what was gonna do it." She told me that she, Courtney, and Dadi were supposed to be in Courtney's truck going down the road when the house exploded, and they would be at Kim's house for a week of rest and relaxation. She said that is what Dadi needed. Then, upon their return they would drive up and see the house was gone. All would be wonderful as the house would be gone and no more worrying about how to pay for it. She went on to say it was much too stressful for my father.

I asked her if she didn't think that someone would call them (the homeowners) and tell them that their house had burned, and she said no, that wasn't a part of her plan. Mother had also given away and sold things in the weeks prior and moved certain items, savable items, to their shed in preparation of this event. She told me the entire situation stemmed on having a foundation. She had heard on TV that if you have a foundation that is the result of a disaster, the government would pay you $600 per month to live in your new home. None of it made sense. She claimed if she burned this home up, the insurance company would pay and she would have the down payment for another smaller mobile home that cost less, and the government would pay them to live in it, which she referred to as a reverse mortgage. She had it all planned out. I tried to explain to Mother that she didn't have a foundation, as they lived in a mobile home, and that I really didn't know what she was talking about.

Meanwhile my dad and Courtney are standing nearby and I can see the look on my Dadi's face. He is mortified as to what she had done and what she had planned. He asked her, screaming, why she didn't tell him she was going to do this. I don't recall her answer, and I'm not even sure she had one. I just kept asking Dadi if he was ok, and he kept referring to his defibrillator in his chest. He said it would just shock him and he'd be ok. The more I lit into Mother asking her about her plan, the more upset Dadi got at me and asked if this was necessary and if we had to do this all day long.

This wasn't something that was just gonna go away; this wasn't a "my bad" or an "oops." I reminded him how many lives Mother had put in danger and that she was a risk to not only herself but Dadi, and it was not safe for her to be there anymore. "What are we supposed to do?" I asked. "Let you both come live with us so she could put us in jeopardy, our children, and let her burn our houses down too?"

Courtney said she needed to run to town to get some medicine, and Mother said she needed to use the restroom and she would go with her. Dadi and I stayed at the house, having the same conversation with just hurtful words, and even though I knew they were like daggers to his heart, I just couldn't let this go.

The Red Cross arrived and comforted me and Dadi. He let one of the ladies into the house while I stayed in the van with the other lady. I answered what standard questions that I could about Mother and Dadi. After touring the house, Dadi came and answered questions for them that I couldn't. My phone rang when Dadi was answering as to what had happened, but before I got out of the van, I heard him say to them that they were all in Courtney's truck.

Then Mother announced that she had forgotten her little red purse that Courtney had bought her, so Dadi went back inside to retrieve it. She had sent my Dadi, her husband, back into the house that she knew she had just set fire to! She left their pets, two dogs and a cat, inside to fend for themselves. Dadi told the Red Cross that upon entering the house, "it was ablaze." Those were his exact words! I wish I could have heard the rest of the conversation, but my husband called and I exited the van and went and sat inside my truck to speak to him. No words could describe what was happening. How do you move through something like this? At some point Mother and Courtney arrived, and the ladies comforted Mother. I didn't get to hear Mother or Courtney's accounts of what happened that day.

When everyone was finished with the Red Cross, we kind of all looked at each other like, now what? I knew Dadi needed to eat, so I took everyone to lunch. Seems odd, but this wasn't a family lunch. The events that had happened had stressed us all and we needed to eat to get through the next stage of events. Courtney and I both decided to take our trucks as not to leave hers at their house with the suitcases in the back. Dadi rode with me and Mother with Courtney. I asked where we should go; my mind was so preoccupied with the fire that I couldn't think of anywhere that was close. Dadi stated that we should go to Cotton Patch, as that was Mother's favorite. I told Dadi in the truck alone (sarcastically) how ironic that we would go to Mother's favorite, as if to reward her for intentionally setting fire to the house. I thought in my head how screwed up this was, how Mother always got her way, and wondered sadly if this was really my life.

Along the way, I told Dadi how after all these years of

heartache, I prayed, "God, please let me have been switched at birth." Dadi asked if I knew how much this hurt him and I knew it did, but I couldn't keep the words from exiting. Having her be a part of me hurt right then, and it was so hard to cope and much harder to understand! I told him I just wished I could take her blood out of me and only have his. "I would rather be only half a person and it be your blood, than be a whole and be part of her." Thinking back now, there are so many times when I shared my heart with my Dadi, and it fell on deaf ears—he just couldn't understand. His rose-colored glasses kept her in his sight as his true love. I know this is horrible to say and especially to my Dadi, but for most of my life I have dealt with countless situations that felt just like this one with Mother.

Upon arrival at Cotton Patch, while Dadi, Courtney, and I discussed whether or not we would be able to eat, Mother relished in the excitement of being able to order shrimp and fish like she did on their anniversary. I looked at Courtney as if Mother was insane, because to me right then, she was. Dadi told her she could only order that if we let him pay, alluding to his feeling that the meal was expensive. "You are not paying!" I objected. "Your house just burned down for Christ's sake!" With hesitation, and in total defeat, he agreed he would not pay. Throughout it all, Mother continued her excitement about this out-to-eat experience. Through the entire course of the meal, I had bouts of emotional crying spells, meltdowns you might say, and even though I was sitting right across from Mother, she never noticed or acknowledged my hurt.

At one point, Courtney grabbed my chin and turned my face directly at Mother, and Courtney told her to look at me and see what she had done, how bad this had upset everyone. Courtney told Mother that she needed to understand that this had a global effect on everyone in the family. Mother was unconcerned, oblivious to the day's events and the results thereof. This was Mother's normal reaction: numb, uncaring, unconcerned. Today would prove to be just another day.

Dadi had several calls with the mortgage company, the Red Cross, and the insurance company during lunch. Each one upset him. We left after Mother finished her meal and went to the motel that the Red Cross had set up for them for two nights. It made me sick knowing they were paying for them to have a place to stay, but if for no other reason, Dadi needed somewhere to lay his head.

Kim arrived at the motel much sooner than she should've, telling me she drove much faster than she should have. The realization that another life was put in jeopardy by Mother added to my anger. We went to their room, and everyone continued drilling Mother as to what she was thinking, then drilling Dadi as to whether or not he was going to make an insurance claim. We discussed over and over the fact that Dadi knew it was wrong, and he just kept saying that if insurance didn't pay, he didn't know what they were going to do.

Dadi said he was willing to take the blame and go to jail. "In jail at least I will get three meals a day, a place to sleep, and I will no longer have to worry about my bills."

I sat crying, broken, like glass in the ocean, knowing that Dadi allowed himself to be the biggest victim in all of this. Yet again, Mother would ruin his life. How much stress could she continue to put on him? How many more bodies would we allow in the wake of her destruction?

We girls decided to leave and go to our homes and let Mother and Dadi sleep on it and hopefully do the right thing come morning. I hugged Dadi and told him I loved him and how truly sorry I was.

It was my hope that he screamed and yelled at her, though his heart was so soft to her I doubt it. He was hurt and in disbelief as were we, but it always came back to protecting her. She was numb, quiet, unconcerned, and carefree. Looking back now, I don't think she could comprehend what she had done, though the level of proudness that she alluded to when we talked was quite disturbing.

I can remember trying to process all of this while trying to recover from a traumatic brain injury. Shortly after Kimberley had come to live with us is when this took place. My brain injury was still fresh, and on a good day I had severe trouble processing things. I had trouble with my balance, my lungs were damaged, and being inside their house with the charred remains made it even harder for me to breathe. Kimberley and I had the joy of cleaning up our parents' mobile home, trying to rescue what we could; however, most everything was a loss, ruined. It was now a picture of the "home" it represented. Oftentimes when we feel as though we're the ones that should be rescued, God places us in a position to do the rescuing.

We children are called to *parenthood* when we least expect it, and at the most inopportune times.

We were seeing what all we could salvage from the kitchen when Kimberley grabbed a charred plate and threw it into the living room wall in a fit of fury. "What an amazing feeling!" She did it again and looked at me with a huge smile on her face, saying, "Do it!" Initially, I looked at her as if she had lost her mind, then, thinking of all my rage and just how things were so out of control, I did it too! And then I did it again! For a few moments, we looked for charred things and chunked them, sometimes even finding semicharred things, chunking them as well as the feeling we received from hurling things into the wall greatly outnumbered the thing's value. We received a huge amount of relief!

Dadi walked in and was horrified at what we were doing. Hours before, the things we were chunking had been their belongings. These things represented their "home." I said, "Dadi, do it. It will help relieve some tension!" He looked at me angrily and was horrified at the thought, but with hesitation, he did!

For a moment, we all three received temporary satisfaction at such a simple release of frustration. It was not lasting. We couldn't help but feel sadness, despair, anger, and disbelief, and we lacked hope. We wiped tears with hands covered in soot. I still feel as if I am trudging back into the fire, leaking flammable memories. I still feel engulfed, and the fire is still hot. I am so saddened. I hope you, the reader, know that I feel sadness and not hatred toward these things and the actions of my mother.

Digging through the remains, we found things that confused us, and even today, we stand in awe of things we found as we cleaned up the charred house. Did Mother snort Bibles? Pills were crushed inside books to be hidden from our eyes. Socks weren't filled with feet but pills. Everything was filled with pills. Pain pills, pain patches, and narcotics were everywhere we looked, tucked in and behind everything. She thought she had hidden them well, but after so many episodes and so many incidents, we knew where to look; we knew her habits, we knew her tricks. Some things she just couldn't outsmart us on. Feeling betrayed, feeling defeated, I remember thinking how I wanted to cover her entire body with those patches. That's what you want? Well, here you go.

Enough was enough; this was the final straw. We knew at this point only God could make beauty from the ashes, and we knew Dadi was Mother's biggest ally and we three sisters were not.

❤

God, only You know the conversations that went on in that motel room after we left. I can only imagine even though as much as Dadi always supported Mother, that this was a little over the top. This was a day that I had to truly trust Your plan for our lives.

From my heart to yours:

- Does your life ever seem unreal and totally out of control?

- Have you ever had to do the right thing, but it seemed so wrong?

My prayer for you:

My prayer is that you never, ever have to live this chapter. It's a lot to take, and even more to understand when your mother intentionally sets fire to her home. This was a time when He truly had to keep our eyes above the waves as at some moments drowning seemed like an easier answer. It was also a time when we inhaled question and exhaled disbelief, and I pray you never experience these feelings. Our saving grace was that only He could bring beauty from the ashes.

His healing words to your heart:

"Indeed, we felt we had received the sentence of death. But this happened that we might not rely on ourselves but on God, who raises the dead" (2 Corinthians 1:9).

Chapter 15:

Sisters Becoming One

Though one may be overpowered,
two can defend themselves. A cord of three strands
is not quickly broken. —Ecclesiastes 4:12

We shared a secret, we lived a secret, yet we lived. We subtly had the same look of "shared understanding." We were like a chain of paper dolls, hands linked, shoulder to shoulder, connected by our hearts. Mother definitely was the missing link. We would never know how it felt to have our arms linked with hers. Yet we had a circle of grace bound by anchored hope!

My sisters and I became unified, as if beating and bleeding from one heart. Nothing was much stronger than three women passionately believing the same way. We were called for one purpose: stopping our mother's addiction! She was conniving—the queen of manipulation—and we knew the only way to survive was for us to stick together. Our lips were laced with tears. We were three girls bound together by one woman, one heart that beat in her chest.

No matter what happened on our journey, nothing could separate us from our common thread. Our stories were intersected by the blood that ran through our veins. We weren't three stories after all—we were one. We would not be quiet in hopes of helping the silent one who lay with her hand upon her chest, feeling her heart beat, longing for her mother's touch. Tears hit my pillow before I even knew I was crying. I didn't want to hurt anymore, and neither did they. We were fractured, we were broken. Three girls united meant there was a line drawn in the sand, us versus Mother and Dadi, and this hurt profoundly.

> *Then they cried out to the Lord in their trouble, and he delivered them from their distress. —Psalm 107:6*

❤

Lord, only You know how hard this was for us—uniting against our parents. At the same time we joined, we also created a huge separation with them, causing so much pain for us all. No matter the reason, right or wrong, when something like this happens, if you have a heart, it hurts.

From my heart to yours:

- Who has God placed in your life: a spouse, a sibling, a friend? Don't go it alone.
- Do you have a mentor for support, or could you be a mentor for someone?

My prayer for you:

I pray you always find yourself linked hand in hand with Him. His circle of grace feels amazing when your hands and hearts grow weary. Don't go it alone. Find a hand; there's an empty one just waiting for yours.

His healing words to your heart:

"Consider it pure joy, my brothers and sisters, whenever you face trials of many kinds, because you know that the testing of your faith produces perseverance. Let perseverance finish its work so that you may be mature and complete, not lacking anything" (James 1:2–4).

Chapter 16:
Giving Up

*We can use our stories to heal our past and to
change our future.*"*—Claire J. De Boer*

I realize now that along the way I was killing myself! I was
killing who I was and who I had been. We are maimed by the
choices we make and have made, by what others do and have
done to us, and by our heavenly Father. He cripples us so He
can heal us. *Thank You, God, for restoring us piece by piece. I
pray we never stop being grateful for Your restoration.*

Oftentimes when we are bent and broken, we don't want the
"right now"—we want the "before" or the "after." Sometimes,
or maybe even frequently, it's easier to give up and end the pain
in whatever method that means. Countless times I wanted to
shout, and more than once I did say: "I give up! I'm tired! I
can't do this anymore! Rescue me please!" But in that same
breath, I didn't want people to know I was so desperate that I
needed saving. That's when, ironically, I knew I wasn't strong

enough to give up. At that point I knew if I gave up, I would also be giving in. I knew my knees had not been on the ground long enough to just throw in the towel.

God would've looked at me and laughed. He knew I was stronger than I appeared, and for that I am forever grateful. He would show me I was. (I'm guilty of going through a storm and reacting as if I'm in a boat casting and trolling when really, I need to sit on the bank, toss out my line and bobber, and wait on Him.) He knows the crushing weight of all our tragedies, and He loves to make a way when there's not one. He was waiting for me to give up; He just didn't want me to give in. All He wanted was for me to relinquish the reigns and let Him be in control, for so many times I told Him, "I've got this," to His dismay and to my heartache. He proved to me that I cannot fix myself, then or now.

God breaks us when we are already *broken*.

Let Him guide you. Is your hope broken? Let Him into the broken places, the broken spaces, no matter how many or how few, how large or how small. Let Him nestle Himself into them all. God wants to live in the holes in your heart that have been void for so long; He can fill places that you don't even know are empty. He presses things in and on our hearts so we'll give them to Him. He's there for us when we pray with unwavering determination, which frankly on some days wavers more than not.

There is beauty in handing over those reigns when your hope is sunk. Sometimes we kneel because we can no longer stand.

His love for us is huge and gentle at the same time. His love is intentional as are our problems, trials, hurts; they are not a mistake to Him. Let Him help you walk through and not around them. He knows the plans for our lives. Remember: He is the Author of our lives, so let Him pen you; let Him spill ink and His blessings on you. Let your story and His collide. He is a great Creator.

What brings you to the cross? Lay it down at His feet.

- Sickness

- Pain

- Divorce

- Disease

- An unplanned pregnancy

- A wayward child

- Elderly parents

- School

- Your job or lack of a job

- Finances

- Depression

- Anxiety

- Despair

- Grief

♥

Lord, thank You for taking our burdens and easing our loads. Thank You for the cross. Thank you for breaking me and completing me and washing me in Your mercy. Thank You for showing me I can't do it on my own. Show us, Lord, daily that we need You.

From my heart to yours:

- What have you given up on that you shouldn't have?

- What have you laid at the cross that you picked back up?

Give it back to Him.

- What brings you to the cross today?

My prayer for you:

How many times did I try to go it alone? I thought I could handle all my problems and I could fix them. Oftentimes we are hard-pressed to pick up what we just laid at His feet. My prayer is that you leave it there. This is His provision for you, for me, through the cross. The cross was enough for the breath you can't take because you are so overwhelmed and burdened! You are not alone; He is waiting there for you.

His healing words to your heart:

"God is our refuge and strength, an ever-present help in trouble. Therefore we will not fear, though the earth give way and the mountains fall into the heart of the sea" (Psalm 46:1–2).

Chapter 17:
Spoken Words and Words Not Spoken

When you stand and share your story in an empowering way, your story will heal you and your story will heal somebody else. " —Iyanla Vanzant

For years, I spoke of my grief, my aloneness, my unhappiness … *just without words.* My face, my body, and my demeanor exposed the sadness within as sorrow mingled down my weakened frame. Pain is often expressed by our physical bodies, and mine was no different.

Pain is a different story for all of us,
from short story to novel, and for some it's
a story that we never allow to be written.

Oftentimes the evidence of our inner feelings and damage

shines outwardly for all the world to see, and these gaping wounds are not pretty. The more we try to cover up, the more we expose, and I often had to walk around with an awkward smile in hopes I wouldn't draw attention to how I really felt inside. I sit here now with this same scenario playing out with migraines. For years, I welcomed stress as if we were dear, intimate friends. I let grief and sadness consume me and control me and almost kill me. I truly thank God that Jesus came for the sick as I was one of them. It took the doctor's words that this behavior was killing me, and I had a decision to make in order for me to become healthy. And I thank God I did. I'm so thankful for the doctor who was God's vessel that day; the words he spoke to me changed my life and I'm forever grateful.

Words change us: they change our lives, they move us and encourage us, they bring us laughter, hope, grace, mercy, and stillness, they bring honor to Jesus, and they bring us closer to Him. They may also bring sadness, despair, hurt, dishonor, shame, or repentance. *"I love you" or "I hate you" have majorly different meanings behind them, and sometimes they are spoken by the same person. "Marry me" comes out of the same mouth that says, "I want a divorce."* Words have meaning. Words matter, every last one of them.

You may eloquently pen a note and place it in the mail (my sister Courtney is one of the most thoughtful, compassionate writers of handwritten notes I know), or you may wake the one next to you with a gentle, "Good morning," but words matter, no matter how many or how few. Words build and words break. You may be the only one on any given day that shows up to flow love to a person. So show love, and flow love.

God writes on our hearts, and we're so special to Him. I am His, and He has connected with me just like a puzzle piece. The closer we get to Him, the closer He snuggles in, leaving us feeling so safe. And if we wander, He brings us back to Him.

He knows our dreams, our hurts, our secrets, our struggles, and our weaknesses.

The further away I get from my past, the more of a blank page there is. Even though things have been seared into my memory, I watch as my past slips further away, knowing it helped to create my present and my future. We are who we are, and we all have a story. What's yours?

Oftentimes, especially as women and little girls, we just want to be heard. We don't necessarily want others to speak in return—just listen. Often, what we say doesn't even demand a response; it's just the act of getting it off our chest, or better yet, out of our gut. However, from experience I know that sometimes the pain is more easily swallowed than spoken. What do you need to say, or better yet, who do you need to listen to? I believe open ears can open hearts, and open hearts can change everything!

❤

If I ever said "I hate you" I didn't mean it and for all the times I said "I love you" I meant it so many more than I ever spoke.
We don't realize that words are so strong.
Remember sticks and stones may break my bones,
but words can never hurt me?
Words can and do hurt us,
spoken words and the lack of certain spoken words as well.
Choose your words carefully.
There are so many to choose from,
make your words count.
Words are so easy to say, but much harder to take back.
You can never totally erase the words
you say from someone's memory.

From my heart to yours:

- What words would you write in the "margins" or what would you go back and mark in red?

- What if you could write just one word for your life, what would it be?

- What would you tell yourself if you were the only one listening?

- Who can you write a handwritten note to? Do it today or get in the habit of doing it often.

My prayer for you:

What's written on the tablet of your heart? I hope the words that have seared you are few, and I pray the words you speak and the words spoken to you show love and healing, not hurt and shame. Words should leave us breathless, not take our breath away.

His healing words to your heart:

"He will cover you with His feathers, and under his wings you will find refuge" (Psalm 91:4).

Chapter 18:
Rejection

He heals the brokenhearted and binds up their wounds.
—Psalm 147:3

I had their look of disappointment memorized (mother and Charlie, ex-husband). My sense of failure doubled; I wasn't good enough to be a daughter or a wife. My ex confirmed what I always knew, but never gave voice to. I had become silent, I had lost my voice, and embarrassment mingled daily for who I'd become and who he was compared to who he had been. I felt small and broken, and my heart had been shattered, destroyed without a drop of blood being shed. I was a testimony that the most hurtful hurts don't involve blood or even physical wounds.

I am a people pleaser and I hate displeasing anyone, especially those I hold most dear. How is it that I wasn't good enough for my own mother and husband? Why did people want me to fit their expectations? Why must I be compared?

Why was I not good enough just as I was, just how He created me?

Perfection puts on a mask. It hides hardships, and pushes struggles beneath the rug. It builds walls of isolation. ... I'm not interested in building walls. I'm more interested in tearing them down. — Shalene Roberts

I didn't want to be just like everyone else to fit in; I'd rather not fit. I am His masterpiece, and I will embrace that. I would bring glory to God by remaining true to His design. I would place my hand on my chest, feel the beat, and know He put it there. I am His, and I am pleasing to Him. I am enough to Him, just as I am. He loves me. I would no longer let people dictate *who I was* and *who I should be.*

As a wife, I struggled with this question: if I changed everything I was to please him, what if he didn't like me when I changed? What if I sacrificed who I am for him, and it wasn't good enough? When would my good enough ever be good enough for him? He would always hold the carrot beyond my reach. He would always want better than I am. I was meant to walk two by two, not alone.

Sometimes I just wanted to live in the gray, the vanilla, the quiet, the alone. Oftentimes I just wanted to walk—far—looking straight ahead as if either side were black or not visible. But I was afraid. What stopped me? It was the not knowing what was ahead. How would I know when to stop? Would it be when the feeling came back, or when the numb went away?

One day I reflected on a day years ago when I entered our front door as a teenage girl, basking in the day's events, longing to share them with Mother, only to find her behind a locked door, and I realized then I had been stripped of my joy. The alcohol and drugs had won again, and losing and all the feelings that accompanied it came rushing back. If my joy was gone now, how could I give it to *my* daughter? The odds were high that the best part of me had been ripped away and if I didn't quickly take hold of myself, the me I had left would be gone forever.

I am so very grateful that God looks at our insides; He knows us inside and out. We are perfect to Him. We are as individual as our fingerprints. He created us. He created you, me, us, everything, and He is still creating today. He allowed me to create the most beautiful, purposeful girl who I will pay His love forward to until I draw my last breath. He created me to love and be loved.

Let Him create you. He is the *master builder.*

I had tried for so many years to be strong and hold my marriage together, but I was growing faint. I was tattered, my health was fading. I was tired of lying lifeless under the weight of my life's love story as I was getting closer to "The End" than "happily ever after." The look of our quilt that his grandmother made for our wedding represented our marriage at our current state. The quilt, too, was tattered and ripped, possibly beyond repair, just like us.

I knew I had to become strong enough to let him go. We were keeping each other broken, and if I let go, I could allow God to mend our pieces, individually. God is the only one who could transform us into whole, separate, beautiful stained glass that could provide beauty to others if mended. Ironically, when we think things are falling to pieces, they most likely are just falling into place, just like His plan, just in His timing. I knew I couldn't hold him up much longer, and I surely didn't want to hold him down. He deserved to be happy, whatever that meant, and I certainly knew I was no longer the one who would make that happen.

God interrupts our lives!

Sometimes God says, "Enough is enough! You are done going down this road," and this was one of those times. I never trusted Him like I did at that point. I was learning to trust Him with everything in me! This was no longer about me, it was no longer about us—it was totally about *Him* and His plan!

This is when God would take me at my weakest and begin making me strong. I would now extend myself grace, so I would be able to extend grace to others, you included. Why is it we can't extend ourselves the same grace that we without hesitation extend others? So many times, I would be so hard on myself, and Kimberley would gently and lovingly point me in the direction of Jesus. I can't tell you how many times I stood in the shadow of her faith. She always told me how important I was to Him and how much I mattered to Him. In so many quiet nights, this is what got me through.

> *He gives strength to the weary and increases*
> *the power of the weak. —Isaiah 40:29*

Don't beat yourself up, love yourself; He made you perfect. Work on seeing yourself through His eyes. I would now take all the cruel words spoken and lay them at the cross; they were His now, not mine. Though I felt lifeless, giving this to Him proved to be very freeing. I spoke these words out loud: "God, I need a miracle!" And then I barely uttered, "I need a miracle," and began to cling to Him like a woman drowning.

When is the perfect or appropriate time to say something to someone that will change everything, that will change their whole world forever? This is what I continued to ponder. I knew I was getting stronger every day. I would listen to God and fulfill His plan for me.

God would take the darkest part of my life and make it shine. He would see me through!

I needed *her* now! I needed him now! I couldn't wait until they needed me. I thank Him that His mercy and healing prevailed.

> *"For I am going to do something in your days that you would never believe, even if someone told you." —Acts 13:41*

There is beauty in the confirmation! Jesus confirmed that day, and He provided. He basically told me, "My love for you is immeasurable." At the end of the day, I won and He won! I get a fairy-tale ending and He gets the glory. God gave me the wisdom and courage to take that first step and move forward. He told me I could either show up or give up; I chose the first. Forgiveness doesn't make what they did right, but it gives my heart healing. It gives me the ability to pray for them.

> *"But I tell you, love your enemies and pray for those who persecute you." —Matthew 5:44*

It is incredibly hard to forgive those who aren't sorry and be ok with never getting an apology or witnessing any feelings of remorse, but when you truly can get to the point where you pray for those who have wronged you, your life will change! You can't imagine the feeling unless you've experienced it by coming before the I AM with those who have injured you the most and truly praying for them. I can't help but believe that some of God's greatest blessings have been initiated by a simple prayer for those who may be the most undeserving.

This is one of my all-time favorite quotes:

> *What if I fall? Oh, but my darling,*
> *what if you fly! —Erin Hanson*

I sit here now just thinking, "What if I had never stepped out in faith? Oh, the blessings I would've foregone." I didn't fail, I didn't fall! Even if I had, I know now that God was there to catch me. If you don't try, you'll never know. I'm flying now, because He gave me wings.

I'm so thankful I didn't become who Mother was. She didn't define me, she didn't label me, and she didn't ruin me! God created us all (including Mother) as His perfect masterpieces, and becoming the true person He created us to be should always be something we strive for and will always take a daily effort.

A successful man is one who can lay a firm foundation with the bricks that others have thrown at him. —David Brinkley

❤

Thank You, God, for Your intervention, Your interruption, Your grace, and mostly for Your mercy! Lord, I thank You that everyone who crosses our paths either molds us or breaks us, bends us, or shapes us. Thank you for these people, and thank You for Your Hand in all of it.

From my heart to yours:

- Who has broken your heart? *Begin genuinely praying for them, and your life will change.*

- How have other people's rejection impacted your life?

- Do you wear a mask to not feel rejection's sting?

- What calls you forward? What calls you to take that next step?

My prayer for you:

He interrupts our lives, and I pray you let Him! It is only through His intervention that we are healed. Don't ever dim your light so others will love you or even like you—you were meant to shine. Even the smallest flicker can be seen and be an inspiration to others. Every breath you take matters to Him!

His healing words to your heart:

"We are hard pressed on every side, but not crushed; perplexed, but not in despair; persecuted, but not abandoned; struck down, but not destroyed" (2 Corinthians 4:8–9).

Chapter 19:
The Mender and the Mending

In all thy ways submit to him, and he will make your paths straight. —Proverbs 3:6

For years, on most days I appeared fine, happy, and normal. On the outside, I looked and seemed as if everything was ok. Few knew where I "lived." Few knew the hurt I felt and the sorrow and sadness I harbored inside. No one could see my heart had been sliced in two and I was slowly dying inside.

Some days I had conflicted emotions, feeling I had every right to hate her, to hate him. Or did I? Mother's betrayal colored me with sadness, and sadness is a much better word to describe how I felt as a daughter and wife than hate. Hate is never what I felt. I was sad, truly sad, consumed with sadness.

This book isn't about justice and revenge; it's about mending hearts, both the offender's and the victim's, both yours and mine. It's about providing encouragement for those going through their own battles. How big or how small your battle is, is in the eye of the beholder. One's war is another's refuge. Some people's storms are so big that even death seems an easier option.

It's hard to forget, yet at the same time it's hard to remember the person before the thirst consumed her, before the liquor became stronger than the shared blood that ran through our veins.

> *Blood* is thicker than water, but I'm guessing that's not true for alcohol.

I realize now that she had a choice to make between her drugs and her daughters, and she chose the one that benefitted her most. I didn't want to hurt anymore. I wanted to be someone who made it through—even if that meant a slender victory, *with* or *without* a mom, *with* or *without* a husband.

Most of the time, the things that matter the most to me are free, and the things I have always desired—the things that sustain me the most—cost me nothing. Give me a little and I will give you tons! It is very easy to love me! My demands are small.

There were people who dug in, broke me open, felt my pain, and extended their hands to me when I had fallen. And now strong, I will extend my hands to others as well (hence the writing of this book). For these people I am truly, truly grateful.

> When God sends people, *welcome* them.

Open wounds can open hearts. We must look for those who are hurting. Shared pain brings people together. This is how the world should work: people helping people, people mending hearts and gaping wounds. If we all helped and healed others, more than we hurt them, this world would be a different place. Believe me, I am preaching to myself as much as I'm preaching to you. I am far from perfect and know where I fail Him and others.

Carry each other's burdens, and in this way
you will fulfill the law of Christ. —Galatians 6:2

If we all just helped *one* person, we could change the world; we should give much more than we take from this earth. I pray after you read the last word in this book that you'll begin looking for that *one* person.

We should all be a constant flow of extending and receiving *grace* to ourselves and others.

I tried over and over to survive by myself, alone, but the beauty came when I leaned on others, family, friends, community. I'm so very grateful to those who helped me carry the pieces of my broken heart as I could never have carried them alone. We carry every little piece to His place of refuge. When we reach to others, they reach back—when we get on their level. Just like when we are trying to get a toddler to walk, we extend our hands out to them, telling them we are here for them, and it's ok to take a step. Likewise, it's ok to walk at a toddler pace sometimes. Just keep putting one foot in front of the other. We're their safety net, and they must trust us. Sometimes as moms we need to hold on, and sometimes we need to let go. I think my mother just "let go" forever, never remembering to extend her hand to me again. So many of those we love forget to look back and see that they have let go of the anchor that would have kept them grounded.

I love this saying:

> *So, we lead and we limp. And there's love*
> *for us in either state. —Kelley Nikondeha*

Just the picture of us limping while others are still following is such a great picture of compassion, friendship, family, teamwork, community.

I love the thought of us leading with love and being led by love. You don't have to be perfect to lead or to follow. We love those who mend, and we love those who need mending as sometimes our feet and faith slip. Aren't we glad He's there to catch us all?

So many of us have experienced and felt *left* instead of *met*. This is exactly how I feel with Mother, but it's because of His mercy that I don't feel it with my heavenly Father.

> *"Can a woman forget the baby at her breast and have no*
> *compassion on the child she has borne? Though she may forget,*
> *I will not forget you!" —Isaiah 49:15*

Lord, I'm so thankful you met me where Mother left me. Help
me heal more than I hurt. Send me that one person and let me
be the "one" for them. Lord, help us cling to You on the way
down and grasp Your Hand on the way up. Thank You for
meeting us and mostly for mending us.

From my heart to yours:

- Are you leading or limping? Does your heart need mending or do you need to mend someone else's heart?
- Who can your "one" person be?
- Have you ever felt *left* instead of *met*?

My prayer for you:

The Lord mends the hearts of offenders and victims alike. May we truly be a constant flow of extending and receiving grace to others and ourselves with every breath we take. He is the God who restores, and I pray you will let go and let Him pursue you. Surrender all you are—lifeless, motionless, breathless—to the ultimate Healer.

His healing words to your heart:

"No weapon forged against you will prevail, and you will refute every tongue that accuses you" (Isaiah 54:17).

Chapter 20:
The Little House on Brown Street

Now to him who is able to do immeasurably more
than all that we ask or imagine, according to his power
that is at work within us, to him be glory in the church
and in Christ Jesus throughout all generations, for ever
and ever! Amen. —Ephesians 3:20–21

Taylor and I transitioned from her "home" for the past fifteen years—the only home she'd ever known, a place of normalcy—to a place that would have to gain her trust. I was having to gain her trust as well, as I had just rocked her world. I spoke words to her daddy that literally took the breath from her.

Our "transition house" was a charming little house at the corner of Brown and Elm, with a front porch light that was so welcoming. It became the place that when we drove up at night and saw that light, I knew it was home. Our front door was adorned with vintage crystal doorknobs, and our garage roof was frequently adorned with a precious little roadrunner who quite often makes himself known across the street at my work. God and my dear friend Dolly provided just what we needed at the very moment we needed it.

Our hardwood floors were unsteady, due to their age, and they constantly tested my balance or lack thereof. We had the most precious stairs that led to our front door that won one evening when I was heading out. I have a permanent scar from falling down the stairs—a continual reminder of the little house on Brown Street and God's amazing grace.

Outside my bedroom window was a beautiful tree, in a not-so-beautiful backyard. Beauty is, however, what we make it, and it was quite beautiful to me on some very dreary mornings when I would wake up and look out the bedroom window. Our backyard was where the cardinals flew, and mama kitty had her kittens.

Well, this tree leaned—far. Oftentimes, I looked at the tree, wondering how old it might be and what its story was. How many people had lived in this charming house built in the 1940s? How many children must have climbed this tree and rested on its long trunk? What stories had been told on or near it? I sat in awe of it one morning, thinking, "To lean is to stand."

Even though sometimes we may feel as if we are about to fall, leaning is a form of standing and leaning is ok. Sometimes God has to take us almost "down" so we appreciate being "up." Also, who better to rest on during that lean than God Himself? He is always there for us, waiting. Look for Him.

❤

Lord, thank You for this charming house and for precious Dolly. You showed Your grace through creaky floors, mama kitty, and a leaning tree.

From my heart to yours:

- Are you grateful, truly grateful, when He provides?

- Do you look for the beauty in the not-so-beautiful?

- Do you lean on Him? If not, can you start?

My prayer for you:

I pray you learn to lean on Him when standing takes its toll on you. Lord, help us to look to You and know You're there waiting. You're our Rock, responsible for our every breath, and You don't fall. Help us to live in Your grace.

His healing words to your heart:

"You will seek me and find me when you seek me with all your heart" (Jeremiah 29:13)

Chapter 21:
The Benefits of Suffering

*"For I know the plans I have for you," declares
the Lord, "plans to prosper you and not to harm you,
plans to give you hope and a future. —Jeremiah 29:11*

Every time I claim Jeremiah 29:11, I cry. It is so overwhelming to think that He is planning "me" and "you" an amazing future.

I also love the book of Philippians, where Paul is writing from prison. The chapter begins with: "Grace and peace to you from God our Father and the Lord Jesus Christ" (v. 2). I love this—grace and peace, yes, thank you! Please give me that. God pours grace in the midst of our trials as if from a huge pitcher, right over our heads! Paul is writing this from prison, and I struggle with this, from my own couch. He's not done either, with you or with me. I love that He's not done; He's just getting started.

In verse 6 Paul writes, "Being confident of this, that he who began a good work in you will carry it on to completion until the day of Christ Jesus." I truly believe that just like Paul, we are where we are for a reason. Allow God to work in your life, even if you feel imprisoned. Paul advanced the Gospel in spite of his circumstances. Can we? We should. So many of the verses speak of rejoicing and joy! I love those two words.

No matter what happens, I need to conduct myself in a way that is worthy and honoring to Him. No matter what I go through in my life, I need to let people see Jesus! I need to bleed Jesus. I need people to experience God through my life. When I'm put to the fire, I need for people to know that He is how I got here, and He will see me through. I am not suffering by mistake. Do I always do this? No. Do I struggle with this? Yes. I'm still a sinner, saved by grace.

For it has been granted to you on behalf of Christ not only to believe in him, but also to suffer for him. —Philippians 1:29

Our lives are not lived without struggle, chaos, fear, agony, and yes, defeat—much defeat. In each season, find Him. Leaves change, droop, and eventually detach from their branches to lie shriveled on the ground, but spring is forthcoming. He has a plan and He's trying to get you there. We have all struggled just trying to reach His hem. Sometimes He lets us grasp only a thread, and sometimes He engulfs us in His robe. His grace is there for the taking.

I am reminded of the lady in Mark 5, who had suffered for twelve years and didn't push through the crowd to get to Jesus, but merely reached for His hem, and was healed. Jesus sought her out and confirmed her healing. He commended her faith.

And a woman was there who had been subject to bleeding for twelve years. She had suffered a great deal under the care of many doctors and had spent all she had, yet instead of getting better she grew worse. When she heard about Jesus, she came

up behind him in the crowd and touched his cloak, because
she thought, "If I just touch his clothes, I will be healed."
Immediately her bleeding stopped and she felt in her body that
she was freed from her suffering. —Mark 5:25–29

I can't help but think what His hem looked like: ratted, ripped, and shred from the miles He had walked while His hem drug tirelessly. We think we must be perfect to approach Him, yet He heals the sick, the plagued. While you or your clothes may be ripped, shred, scorned, or scoffed, He loves us all the same, so *come as you are.* His grace is sufficient for you and for me. Ask Him to hem you in.

He's saying, "Don't go it alone." There will soon be another season just around the corner. Will you have learned from the one you are in? God tests us, all of us. Let Him use you. I often say that the lesson may not even be yours; you just may be the vessel He is using to teach someone else. Doesn't it feel good to know He wants to use *you*?

We need to let Him use us. God wants us to be His dwelling place. Sometimes we enter a door without even knowing it; we walk into His safety and protection. There's no space that His love can't reach. In the deepest, darkest part of you, He's there.

Sit, stand, or lean and let Him rain on you; let Him restore you. Bask in His mist, His drizzle, or His all-out downpour. Some of our biggest blessings are found in His storms, so rest in Him. There is freedom in the shelter of the Lord. And even though He rescues us to be His lights, sometimes we need to rest in His shadows.

Sometimes He has to move us away from the light for us to see the light. Look for Him in your darkness and He will help you find the light one inch at a time. Even in your darkest place, find Him in the shadow.

Whoever dwells in the shelter of the Most High will rest in the shadow of the Almighty. —Psalm 91:1

Kimberley and Courtney stood in the shadows, and God protected them. He allowed them to make their own choices, sometimes debilitating choices, to bring them back to Him. He sometimes sends us out on those edges to see if we will jump or not, to see just how much we trust Him. It's so easy to tell others to trust Him, but oftentimes trust is debilitating to us, and oftentimes trust is nothing short of paralyzing to me.

Ask Him to draw you closer to Him.

Kimberley often says how when she looks back, she feels heartache to think that when she was nineteen, and Courtney and I were sixteen and fifteen, she got married and left us to fend for ourselves. Although madly in love with her husband, Billy, she had not only been the oldest sister but a maternal figure in so many ways for so long. It was sad for her to think about leaving us behind. One of the happiest times in her life was often tainted by the bitter sting of two sisters at home on their own. How often does the absence of a mother flow through so many aspects of one's life, though some not discovered until years later?

The following is Kimberley's beautiful testimony of God's amazing grace:

God's amazing grace, how sweet the sound. My life is truly His abundant grace and mercy poured over me like a soft flowing river to my soul. God has held my hand and guided me through when sometimes I had no knowledge it was Him at all. I will live my life in a thankful overflow to Him the rest of my days. Not only am I called to this, but I can't help but want others to know how incredibly wonderful my heavenly Father is.

Let me take you back—I was saved at the age of 12 having

gone through confirmation classes at our church. Shortly after that, we moved and I was then trying to find my way, new town, with the challenge of making new friends. Back then, I was 12 but looked 16, taller and let's just say my body matured rather quickly. I have learned as an adult that when I feel out of control it's very uncomfortable to me and therefore I try and control the things I can. So, in that, trying to make new friends and fit in, let's just say I used my assets to what I thought was my advantage. I lost my virginity at 12. Well, I fit in, but in all the wrong ways. I learned to lifeguard, I think at 14. I had a beautiful tan body when we again moved when I was 14½ and again, trying to fit in using my body to do so found myself pregnant at 15. Our mom was in control of the house and decisions therein and ruled us girls with a strong will. Rowe v Wade had been put into action just 2 years prior to this, so the logical thing for my mom was to take me to have an abortion. She ran my then boyfriend off and I continued to try and gain control of my life the only way I knew how, using my body. At the age of 17, I found myself pregnant again. The same situation played out again, with the difference being the boyfriend was my now husband of 38 years. The catch at least in my mom's eyes was he (Billy) was 21 and I was only 17 (a minor). She promptly said she would have him thrown in jail if we did not comply. So, again, I had an abortion. Billy and I dated until I was 19 and then we married. Needless to say, I couldn't hardly wait to have a baby and on our first anniversary I was a month pregnant with our oldest daughter, Misty. Five years later Charlsey came and 3 years later Kelsey. One of the things Mother always told me was that I was too selfish to have more than one child. I'm glad she wasn't right. All our girls were told about my abortions and I have given my testimony many times at youth events, churches, and the pregnancy center where

I volunteered. This was so others could receive the gift of God's grace, mercy, and nonjudgmental, unconditional love. To Him be the glory and honor. Amen.

My sister Kimberley's life verse is found in Matthew 5:16: "In the same way, let your light shine before others, that they may see your good deeds and glorify your Father in heaven."

We know how wonderful things are by how horrible things have been. Without the ugly, we lose our judgment of how beautiful things are.

❤

Lord, I thank You for where You put me, where I landed! If I were sitting on a bed of roses all the time, I wouldn't appreciate the smell of them like I do—and their soft comfort. I would take them for granted. Wow, where I've been, and double wow, where I'm going! May I always be a testimony of Your love and kindness. I will remain in Your hands, moldable, until I see Your face. I am blessed!

From my heart to yours:

- Can you make a stand for Christ? *(In your daily life when things are going good? How about during tough times, through your challenges?)*
- Do you seek Him? Do you allow Him to seek you?
- What season are you in? Are you allowing it to change you?

My prayer for you:

I pray you begin to see suffering as an honor, as He doesn't just choose anyone to go through the fire. Lord I am so grateful that You make something beautiful out of our messes and that You live in the deepest corners of our shame. Teach us to reach for Your hem, as Your grace is there waiting for us. I pray you never take His grace for granted.

His healing words to your heart:

"Blessed is the one who perseveres under trial because, having stood the test, that person will receive the crown of life that the Lord has promised to those who love him" (James 1:12).

Chapter 22:
Praying

Because he bends down to listen, I will pray
as long as I have breath! —Psalm 116:2 NLT

Anyone can pray for anyone or anything without anyone even knowing they are doing it. I love to pray behind the scenes. I love to pray, and my prayer life totally changes me inside if I let it. I have been prayed for by so many wonderful people, and I constantly try to pray forward. Praying is such an easy thing to do for someone. If praying seems hard for you, don't think "praying"—think "talking." It's that easy.

The *bridge* between panic and peace is *prayer*,
so let Him meet you.

God hears the simplest prayers, so pray. I have seen so many prayers answered, and how do you get what you want if you don't ask for it? He wants to provide for you, hear from you, and communicate with you; a Father wants to speak to His children. The secret places in your heart, He knows them, so don't allow the noises of worry and fret to get so loud in your head that you can't hear His voice. Pray. Wait. Trust. He knows your voice, so trust *His*.

Our grandmothers and great-grandmothers went before us and prayed for us, just like we are praying for *our* daughters! Praying mothers are some of God's greatest tools. We're a menace to Satan's work, and this is such a great feeling. Not much will stop a mother who's determined or on a mission. God answers prayers! These women that came before us never got to taste the sweet blessings we received and continue to receive because of their sweet prayers they prayed. Even though they knew they would not have the blessings that we have now, they diligently prayed for us with selfless love. Prayer is such a privilege that God has given us to communicate with Him and Him with us.

I love prayer and totally believe if we talk to God, He hears us. Again, how do you ever expect to receive the things you do not ask for? I have seen prayer work! God has shown me time and time again, and I believe He'll show you. Jesus said, "Ask and it will be given unto you; seek and you will find; knock and the door will be opened to you. For everyone who asks receives; the one who seeks finds; and to the one who knocks, the door will be opened" (Matthew 7:7–8). He tells us to ask and it will be given to us, so why do we not ask? Just remember sometimes His best yes for us is a big fat no.

I can remember Nanny faithfully reading her Bible using a magnifying glass while hummingbirds flew outside her window. Her Bible was large print due to her failing eyesight, and the pages were torn, stained, and tattered. Nanny marked her favorite verses with a blue ballpoint pen and had a piece of paper tucked inside that she listed these verses on. I bought

Nanny this Bible, and Kimberley watched her read it for years while Nanny lived with her family. The decision on who would get her Bible was a difficult one, but Kimberley's grace to me ran deep the day we decided that I would get it.

I still use it today, and it is pieced together with clear packing tape as I have continued its use and therefore further abuse, so to speak. I hope I never forget the day that David and I sat and taped it back together at his desk. I cry just thinking of how much this Bible has been read and written in and how dear it is to so many. It contains so many fingerprints, and I know personally I have tear-stained many a page. God is good.

I can still close my eyes, or quieten my mind, and see Nanny there. Likewise, just now a precious bird is resting in the tree outside my writing desk, peacefully singing me a song while I write about Jesus and Nanny. The Bible was important to Nanny and she made it important to us girls. God is good, really good, and His orchestration of things is incomprehensible most of the time. We should look for Him in everything! God is amongst us always, even in the little things—no, especially in the little things. Find Him in the big and little.

We tried to live the rite of passage without our mother's example as if being tasked to paint someone's face that we'd never seen. There is irony in learning to be a mother from a father (God, my heavenly Father) and in feeling "disgraced" by your mother and feeling "graced" by our heavenly Father. He was with me, with us, along the way every step, guiding us to be the moms we are today. Mother was the best person to chart our paths; she was supposed to stand in the gap for us, like we are doing for our girls! I have prayed so many prayers for Taylor, that God would hold her in His Hands until she is strong enough for Him to gently let her down. I believe He will do this and I trust Him to. I can't even imagine not doing this for her. He has entrusted me with David's babies and grandbabies, and it's my honor to pray for them. Why could my mother not pray these things for me?

The things that were important to me as a little girl became critical when I became a mother. Even little girls know how to nurture their baby dolls. I was the best mommy ever to my babies growing up. I knew what mothers were supposed to be, and that's what I wanted to be. I would connect with my daughter. I would be there for her. Always!

One of my greatest needs was to be connected, both emotionally and physically, with family. I wanted and needed people to love. I am a people gatherer. I love family and friends and friends who are family. I now belong. We now belong! We are loved! We share, by His grace, love and encouragement with those who love and encourage us. We are restored! God provided! I am living my dream! I don't take it lightly and will never stop thanking Him for all I have. For all we have. So many prayers prayed, so many prayers answered! All He wants us to do is ask. All He wants us to do is step out of His way and trust Him. Let Him be there for you. Ask Him to! *Pray! Pray! Pray!* He hears you even if you do not speak out loud. That's how you know He hears our prayers. He will pull you through, time and time again. Just say amen.

> *Prayers turn ordinary parents into prophets who shape the destinies of their children, grandchildren, and every generation that follows. —Mark Batterson, Praying Circles around Our Children*

> *Before you were conceived, I wanted you. Before you were born, I loved you. Before you were here an hour, I would die for you. This is the miracle of life. —Maureen Hawkins*

If everything were wonderful and nothing challenged us, why would we look to Him? Why would we have to trust Him? Why would we have to pray? Personally, I pray the easiest, most childlike prayers ever. If praying is hard for you or if the words won't come, pray more. Anything we do over and over becomes easier as we do it. Make sure before your knees hit the ground your heart has sought Him. I try every morning to pray as I am driving to the office. I want to try and direct my day before it directs me.

❤

God, it's me again … I'm so glad I can talk to you about anything and everything. Sometimes I just need to talk. I need to tell someone how I feel, and You're always there. You never get tired of hearing me. Thank you for listening. I won't go to the office alone; I will never go without you. Help me today to look to You in everything, really everything. I know I do a lot of stupid things, and I know you forgive me, but help me today to honor You—in everything! I hope people see You in me. Most of all thank you for loving me.

I'm *falling* on my knees, God please!

From my heart to yours:

- *What pain and burdens are you carrying?* Sometimes we carry the broken pieces to God, and days or weeks later, we find a shard that we left behind (just like when a glass is broken and we think we have all the pieces picked up and later find out we didn't). Trust Him and lay it down; give it to Him in prayer. Ask Him once, then thank Him.

- What broken piece do you still need to give to Him?

- What keeps you from praying?

- Have you ever *not* spoken a prayer out loud, but it was still answered?
- Who and what can you begin to pray for? *And what can I pray with you about?* Let me join with you in prayer. Email me: shelley@shelleytaylor.net. I wouldn't have survived if it weren't for the prayers of so many.

My prayer for you:

Pray. Wait. Trust. I pray you'll just talk to Him and not stress over the perfect words to pray. Don't make it harder than it is, and believe me, I'm preaching to myself as well. When it's hard to pray, take a breath and remember that's the time we should. He hears our spoken and unspoken prayers no matter how childlike or impressive they are. Sometimes we don't need to speak; we just need to pause and listen. Practice pausing.

I *pray* when His yes is no that it will be followed by His *grace* and you will forever *thank* Him.

His healing words to your heart:

"Rejoice always, pray continually, give thanks in all circumstances; for this is God's will for you in Christ Jesus" (1 Thessalonians 5:16–17).

Chapter 23:
What Takes Your Breath Away

"At this my heart pounds and leaps from its place." —Job 37:1

One of the best pieces of advice I have ever been given was this: "All I can tell you is life is too short to not be happy! Whatever that means for you, you just need to be happy." At this very time in my life, I was feeling drained and empty—breathless—and it's no doubt that God orchestrated those very words for me to hear. I had been living so many moments that I thought I could just stop breathing.

There will be so many people who leave you breathless (both good and bad), but the one who reminds you to breathe is the one to continue your breaths with. Life is indeed too short and our days are numbered. Our tomorrows are not promised and oftentimes are not granted. Happiness in whatever shape or form is waiting for you. He wants your days to be full of joy and contentment, breathless moments that thread to the next.

I love, love! Love is a four-letter word, so use it! I love the thought of "vats" of love and extending and receiving love. I surround myself with positive people and typically have a "Who can I breathe oxygen into today?" attitude. What if we all offered breath to one another like He offers us grace? May you drown in His grace!

❤

Lord, thank You for providing those words that life indeed is too short to not be happy. You knew exactly what I needed to hear at that very moment. You don't promise us tomorrow, so help us to seek breathless moments today.

From my heart to yours:

- Who can you breathe life and love into today?
- Who can you love that's unlovable?
- What takes your breath away?

My prayer for you:

I pray you will make your tomorrows count. When you come within a moment of drawing your last breath, breaths matter. You matter! Lord, help us to be loved, show love, and especially to love the unlovable and spread joy and light in a world that's full of darkness. Help us to seek those things that leave us breathless.

His healing words to your heart:

"I know that there is nothing better for people than to be happy and to do good while they live" (Ecclesiastes 3:12).

Chapter 24:
Worship

*Let me hear joy and gladness; let the bones you
have crushed rejoice. —Psalm 51:8*

Stories behind the most touching songs are written during events that we ourselves would never want to go through, as was this book! People write their experiences hoping to connect with the listener or the reader, to provide hope, help, and healing to both the reader and the writer alike.

There's a singer at church who's part of our worship team, and seeing her on stage (knowing she's about to sing) makes me smile. I know she's going to give it all she has, and we will be blessed because of her efforts and willingness to let God use her. God comes to hear her sing; His presence fills the room. She belts words out, stomps her feet, and occasionally jumps, and we tap our toes, clap our hands, and let tears fall. God is good! I attend an incredible church with amazing God-given pastors and music. It's definitely a wonderful way to feed my soul at the beginning of the week, sitting next to the one I prayed so long for.

I love the sound of God's people singing, wind blowing the leaves on the trees, the crispness of the blown leaves in fall, the rattling of my crosses on my wall, the ocean waves, the thunder, and the sound of children playing. And one of my all-time favorite sounds is the sound of a giggling child. So many things are contagious: yawns, smiles, and laughter.

Lord, thank you for David, who sings in my ear at church. Hearing him provides the most awesome warmth inside just knowing he's there with me. We worship together, and we make the most magnificent team, but he also constantly makes me laugh! His laughter is just a small amount of grace that flows on and through me daily. Just to look at him, you see his eyes crinkle with kindness, and the skin around his eyes is weakened from the years of laughter.

Lord, so many of these things send me into the spirit of worship and worship only leads to Thanksgiving. It only takes the smallest of things to warm my heart and send a tear to my eye. Show us how to jump into the deep end instead of tipping our toes in the shallow. May we sing Your praises and find Your beauty in all we do.

Thanksgiving truly is my most favorite time of the year. I love to sit and reflect on what has been given, what has been taken and God's perfect plan for me and mine.

When I had nothing else to hold onto, I gave God what I had—everything! I offered my open hands to Him. He showed me that if I gave Him my little, though my "everything," He would make it big, ginormous, and plentiful. It's hard to explain to people the greatness of trusting and believing. It is ever so humbling. These are some of the reasons I sing His praises. I will forever worship Him with thanksgiving.

I feel so close to God while listening to people's fingers glide up and down their guitar and fingers dance up and down the piano, worshipping the One who made us. Music is such a blessing and is so near and dear to our family. Some of my and Taylor's closest times have been while worshipping and praising Him together, hands raised, hearts and heads bowed, while tears poured. Some of my fondest memories are of us belting out His praises with people we love, and now I can watch her beautiful ministry: "signing" words of praise. God is good.

> God had to unclench my hands in order for me to raise them to His glory! There is *power*, *freedom*, and *beauty* in the smallest open palm.

I turn on praise songs even when my eyes are weary and tear stained, giving Him the glory through the tough times as well. Oftentimes, it was during my darkest days that I was the most loving and giving to others, wanting them to receive from me what I wanted and couldn't have or wasn't getting. Sometimes just doing for others makes us feel better. I am truly grateful for those who have given so much to me along the way.

> *But I will sing of your strength, in the morning*
> *I will sing of your love; for you are my fortress,*
> *my refuge in times of trouble.* —Psalm 59:16

At church, I stand and sing words of praise either while fighting a battle, just having finished fighting a battle, or awaiting a battle on the horizon. Sometimes I sing, barely voicing words, as I'm overcome with emotion, and the words I plead inside are louder than the words spoken. It's easier to sing, and we may even sing louder when a mountain is not in sight, but we must always walk by faith. Trust Him, let Him renew your strength, watch Him work and sing His praises!

Lord, I thank You for the mountains that force us to look up to You. You scoop us up and help us climb and make us strong enough to look back and see how far we've come. Thank You for never leaving us.

My desire is to stand on the mountaintop and scream how He was faithful. He is faithful when we trust Him. We gave our mother and all her baggage over to Him, and He brought us through. He *can* and *will* do the same thing for you. I gave him my broken heart and broken marriage, and He brought me through. He is waiting to prove His grace, mercy, and faithfulness to you—right now—and His ear is bent, waiting and listening for You to sing His praises. May we never grow weary in thanking Him. To God be the glory. Amen.

His *mercies* are waiting on the other side.

The battle is the Lord's. Trust Him, my friend; trust Him, even if it's a war you didn't start. He is there, He uses storms to change us, and He never forsakes His children. Joy comes in the morning, after the long fight, the tiring battle, when you can no longer stand. Joy is right ahead. Don't stop choosing joy!

Arise [from the depression and prostration in which circumstances have kept you—rise to a new life]! Shine (be radiant with the glory of the Lord), for your light has come, and the glory of the Lord has risen upon you! —Isaiah 60:1

Whatever you're thinking of right now, *give* it to Him.

❤

I totally trusted You. I was willing to lose everything, and You came through for me. You came through for Taylor. You came through for David and me. You went before me, preparing my way and oh how I love You.

From my heart to yours:

- What sends you into a spirit of worship?

- What keeps you from worshipping?

- What are you infecting people with (joy, sadness, anger)?

- Do you confess Jesus Chris is Lord—in every season? Begin today.

- We will all be called to bow before God the Father. Will you be ready?

My prayer for you:

Lord, may we praise You with every breath we're given! Show us how to jump into the deep end instead of tipping our toes in the shallow. May we sing Your praises and find Your beauty in all we do. Even when You don't move our mountain, let us still praise You. Help us to sing in the shadow of the lurking mountain and look to You in times of trouble. May we always raise our hands and our hearts to You and give You the glory.

His healing words to your heart:

"Let everything that has breath praise the Lord" (Psalm 150:6).

Chapter 25:
Sacred Places We Gather

"Come to me, all you who are weary and burdened,
and I will give you rest." —Matthew 11:28

Granny's house was home, not just to us but to anyone who entered, and no one who came in would ever argue this point. A stranger never entered and certainly no one left hungry. Even in my Granny's last years, while she was dying from both Parkinson's and Alzheimer's, she was still feeding people in her head, and she vocalized this often to us.

I just want to pray for a moment for the ones who have dealt with Alzheimer's, for the lack of a better word or words, it is horrible, devastating, and heartwrenching. We have dear, close friends who are living this out, and my heart breaks a little deeper for them each day. To put these words in picture form, our Granny stood close to 5'10 and died weighing around 80 lbs. Mentally and physically, she was unrecognizable.

Illnesses that deal with the brain have been a part of my family and extended family for years. My dad's precious brother killed himself when I was just a little girl, and my mom's dad lost his battle with cancer. We also battled Mother's addiction, Granny's Alzheimer's and Parkinson's, Courtney's Parkinson's, Kimberley's blood clot in her head from falling when she was sixteen, and Taylor's and my brain injuries.

It never gets easy; each new thing brings its own challenges and learning curves. My sister Kimberley said Granny's Alzheimer's bout was the only time she told her daughters to intentionally lie to Granny, just to make her not worry. When she believed helicopters were in her hospital room, you had to duck and take cover under the bed as she truly believed they were there. We "fake" baked cakes for the pretend people who came to visit as this was always so important to her.

We took turns staying with Granny, babysitting her in her hospital room, and at the end of the day, we left completely exhausted, both mentally and physically. I wonder if those were small preparations for the days I would face after my brain injury, totally mentally exhausted at the end of the day.

Food, friends, family, and family gatherings were very important to Granny, and she instilled their importance in us through the years. We entered, as did everyone, through the kitchen door that came in from the garage. Granny always said that family entered through that door, and if we entered there, she would get to see us first as she was always in the kitchen. Only people that didn't know Granny and Gran-Gran came through their front door. Some of my greatest memories growing up were in her kitchen, touching, tasting, and preparing. Her kitchen was one small room, quaint and intimate. I realize now, having my own kitchen, just how small hers was, and just how many things she didn't have. Granny made the most incredible dishes with the most ordinary equipment and food.

At Granny's I was the dishwasher, table setter, stirrer, and more. I watched her in awe, working her magic, wondering and hoping I could be like her someday. We never shared a meal at her table when we didn't say, "Granny, come sit down, we'll clean the kitchen in a bit." Ironically, today I am trying to teach myself to let the dishes be, and share in the fellowship with family and friends. Through the years, I have missed out on so many memories while washing dishes and cleaning up the kitchen. I do have to admit that David is getting good at recognizing this, and he comes to rescue me from the kitchen to join the fun. Why can I not realize that life is shorter than it seems and the dishes can wait until everyone's gone?

I was like a kid in a candy store in Granny's kitchen. The smells were incredible, and I still cook so many of her recipes today for my family and friends and have shared many a recipe along the way. I wonder how many times "Granny's lasagna" has been made by me, my sisters, their daughters, and all our friends we've shared it with. She taught me how to feed others and put others before myself. It is incredibly special to know that way back then God was preparing a pint-sized, brown-eyed girl to be the woman I am today through my Granny's small, quaint kitchen. He knew all along that food and family would be of immeasurable importance to me. I am the wife and mother I am today because of things she taught me about caring, consideration, and compassion when it comes to food and family. She was instilling values and heritage in me that are priceless, and I hope I can pass these down to my grand-children.

Granny was feeding me without even putting food in my mouth, and I was ever so hungry. Her kitchen provided me warmth and love unending and is definitely the first place I began learning to feed my family and friends. It will always be such a special place to me.

Memories are made on spoons. —Shauna Niequist

Share yourself and your traditions and make new memories with each and every dish that you prepare. Learn from each recipe, and make it better the next time. Do it different every time if that's what makes you happy. Sit around your table, even if there's no food on it while kind words are spoken, living, loving, and laughing until glasses are empty and hearts are full.

Come to the table and *taste* of His *grace*

One Christmas we gathered at my table and played poker with Nanny using toothpicks as poker chips. Cry, laugh, and love until your hearts overflow.

Everybody needs beauty as well as bread,
places to play in and pray in, where nature may heal
and give strength to body and soul. —John Muir

One of my most favorite things the "Taylor" family does is have family dinner. Each month, on a rotation basis, each "Taylor" family member and their spouse hosts dinner. It's a tradition that everyone has grown to expect and love. Everyone gets together, even if for a short time, due to homework, sports, and other obligations and shares great food and even greater conversations. It's a way to keep in touch, laugh, love, and live … together. The family time is what matters, not the food, and I encourage you to begin this with your family.

For so many years, I longed for a spiritual leader, someone who thought taking me to church was important. I wanted someone who would take me to Sunday school and sit and learn the Bible with me. Someone who knew that gathering with others and singing and hearing about Jesus were things I needed. I needed someone who believed in prayer and would ask me to pray with him and for him on important things in not only our lives but the lives of our children and others. My husband, David, prays for me, for us, and for our families, and I don't want to live a day that he doesn't.

In David, I've found that someone who loves church like I do and loves worshipping the One who brought us together. That someone helped organize our entire family (children and their children) to go to downtown Fort Worth and feed the homeless. Jesus' entire ministry, His death, and His resurrection showed love to people, and we should walk and live in His image. We made a difference that day. We changed some lives and definitely they changed ours.

My ex-sister-in-law (who will always be more than that title) started a tremendous ministry in downtown Fort Worth and has fed thousands of homeless people (both physically and spiritually). Kay has done more in a short time than I will in a lifetime. God has smiled on www.onewaymission.org for sure. One Way Mission provides emergency assistance, food, clothing, and shelter for low-income families, the poor and downtrodden, and the homeless at risk in southeast Fort Worth, Texas, and wherever God leads them.

David is that someone who loves worship like I do; he loves Jesus, hope, mercy, grace, worship, and healing. Broken and lost people are important to him, because they're important to God. I stand and sing and sit and learn next to him at church, and my heart is full, I am taken back, and my face smiles. We pray that at the end of our last breath that our children and their children will have seen Jesus in us and our lives will have made a difference. God provided my heart's desire; David flows love to me and through me and I am truly blessed. We make a great team! David Taylor, I love you!

When we walk with each other into the sacred, holy places that changed us, when we show each other the raw and wild

parts of ourselves that are still healing, it is a radical kind of
Presence. And sometimes, it is where our world and God's
collide. —Bethany Suckrow

The proper words to thank Him for colliding my and David's worlds will never come. It's an awesome feeling to marry your best friend, for God to totally take you by surprise and change your world and his. To share a bond for years with someone—and then share your words, your family, your breaths, your space with them—is incredible. God provides some of the best surprises. Long story short, God provides.

To David and me, Nocona, Texas, is a place we linger, especially David. He built a house there for dear friends of ours, and he has loved to go and hunt there for years. It's a place of refuge where he can both play and rest, and even when he works, I know it's still restful. It's a place where mornings come early, anticipation grows while sitting in a deer blind, naps are a must, driving the tractor with the grandbabies is a given, and early evening hunting grows his appetite for dinner.

Find something that you *love* and *linger* there.
Rest there if necessary.

Nocona, to me, means quietness, aloneness with God, the most incredible sunrises, and a generous amount of writing in between cooking and watching the grandbabies run amuck. Nocona is small and intimate and hosts tons of nature and wildlife. Sometimes the wildlife is a little close for comfort, but luckily a gun is normally nestled closely by. Not many days go by that we don't long to be there and go there. We normally head out after a busy week and return refreshed and restored, ready to begin again. (Update: since this writing, our dear friends who owned the ranch in Nocona have both passed from this earth to the arms of Jesus. The ranch is for sale, and I pray God's greatest blessings on the new owners. I hope they enjoy it every bit as much as we did.)

❤

Lord, thank You for providing those places to long in, to take rest in. Thank You especially for those people who we can dwell with in the sacred places.

From my heart to yours:
- Where do you *linger*, not just where do you go? What do you *long for*, spend extra time in? Where is *your* space where you can be alone in or alone with Him? Find that place and make it your own and dwell there.

- If you are a caregiver to someone with Alzheimer's, please, please seek out a support group in your area. And please email me (shelley@shelleytaylor.net), and I promise to pray for you. If you have dealt with this, I am so sorry. If you are going through it now, constant prayers for you.

My prayer for you:
Help us to rest in You and know there is room at Your feet to just dwell. Help us to "long" for You and find comfort in Your sacred space. I pray You provide us with people we can gather with and gather around while we wait here for You.

His healing words to your heart:
"You are my hiding place; you will protect me from trouble and surround me with songs of deliverance. I will instruct you and teach you in the way you should go; I will counsel you with my loving eye on you" (Psalm 32:7–8).

Chapter 26:
Love Unwavering

No, in all these things we are more than conquerors through him who loved us. —Romans 8:37

I'm an advocate for love—the ooey-goey, sloppy kiss, hug tightly, walk slowly together, climb in bed exhausted and stay up way too late talking and giggling kind of Love. The kind of love that wakes you with a smile, and as your eyes close and you rest for the night, the same smile lingers on your lips. The glow doesn't end. Love leads and I follow.

God shows me daily that He was faithful and came through when I totally trusted Him, when my faith was finally bigger than my fear. He not only came through for me but He came through for my daughter, Taylor, as well. I am so thankful that He sent Keifer to be the love of her life. Keifer is loved by our family, and he is exactly who God placed in Taylor's life when she so desperately needed him. Taylor had just watched her world cave in and her normal turn to disaster, as I had just divorced her dad, and she needed nothing less than God to "show off" for her—and He did. When I sit and let the thought of both David and Keifer soak in, I cry happy, happy tears, and I realize just how much He loves us. He loves you! Each of us matter like crazy to Him. He knows our names, and I will never stop declaring His praises!

He *loves* us!

David spent approximately thirty years eating popcorn, two to three nights a week, from his Stir-Crazy popcorn machine. He set the bait for my heart with this homemade popcorn, then sealed the deal with his chivalry and charm. In my previous marriage, words that mattered were never spoken, like "I love you" or "You are beautiful." However, David's chivalry is over the top, and I couldn't ask for someone to speak kinder words to me. He tells me he loves me and I am beautiful when I least expect it and when I am so undeserving. We complement each other literally and physically. We make each other better people. We complete each other, and when I feel the warmth of his hand laced in mine, it is a subtle reminder of thousands of prayers that were prayed and answered. Gratefulness overcomes me!

❤

I cannot tell You how honored I am that You chose this life for Taylor and me. Thank You, Lord, thank You for loving us wildly. We are forever grateful for those You sent to love us and those we love. May we always continue to give and receive love to each other along the way.

From my heart to yours:

- He Loves us fiercely, what do you Love fiercely?

- What has He done for you that is beyond your belief, something *only* He could do? *Take a moment and thank Him again for it. Right now.*

- What is something that you can let your *faith be bigger than your fear?*

My prayer for you:

Lord, show them a wild love, a love that is constant and unwavering. Step in and show off in a way that no one can deny it was You, the way You did for Taylor. May their faith be bigger than their fear, these things I pray.

His healing words to your heart:

"Jesus replied, 'You do not realize now what I am doing, but later you will understand'" (John 13:7).

Chapter 27:
When God Winks

But you are a chosen people, a royal priesthood,
a holy nation, God's special possession, that you may
declare the praises of him who called you out of
the darkness into his wonderful light. —1 Peter 2:9

I love going through the days looking for God winks: an answer to prayer that comes at that perfect moment, a small, subtle confirmation that He is involved in the details of your life, a silent little reminder that He's there even when things seem unsure and uncertain—what the "world" would call a coincidence.

If you want to find happy, you can! If you want to find happiness in almost everything, you can! I'd love to challenge you to go through life with a "my cup is overflowing" attitude. If you think that's just beyond your reach, how about doing it for a day, then another? You get it. I believe that we can find something good in almost everything, even the horrible things. I believe God uses the awful, the drastic, the devastation, and the life-changing things to change us! Sometimes God (the ultimate Gardner) has to "till us up," "prepare our soil," "make us ready," and "strip away the old" to prepare us for the new! We have to be ready to receive His blessings!

- When we left the hospice center the night Mother drew her last breath, there was the most amazing sunset when we pulled out of the parking lot—God's confirmation picture to us that she was with Him and was better than she'd ever been.

- Every time Courtney sees a butterfly or flutterby, she says, "That was Dadi." During one of the last days that I worked on the book and I wondered if the finish line was even a possibility, a black butterfly with the most incredible shade of iridescent blue and perfect round yellow spots on its underside landed just outside my writing window. Now, just days later, the same color butterfly is back. Both times I have been typing/editing in the chapter that speaks of my twin. I just ran and told Taylor, and she responded, "Maybe that's your answer." I was overcome with tears.

- I came home from work one day to the most beautiful surprise I had ever been given or gifted. David had lawn people come and plant an extraordinary garden of flowers and roses. Roses always remind me of Dadi as he always had a rose garden and instilled his love for them in me, and through the years pruning them has proved to be so therapeutic. My roses are a permanent "God wink" reminder of both my Dadi and David's love.

- Nanny loved hummingbirds, and Kimberley always has a hummingbird feeder not too far from reach outside on her patio—a reminder of when Nanny lived with her and her family and the wonderful memories they shared.

- We have a family group text, and Courtney is notorious for capturing and sending the most beautiful pictures that remind her of Mother and Dadi. I know tears fall every time as she hits Send.

- We were having Spa Day this past semester of Embrace Grace, and Holly wrote words on rocks to represent attributes and God's provisions for us: *loved, encouraged, provided, valued*, etc. I reached in and grabbed a rock like everyone else, and when I read the word tears began forming and I bit my lip to try and keep them from falling. I was the last one to read their word, and I had succeeded in not crying until Holly asked me to read my word, and I said "protected" while looking in her direction. Holly was overcome with emotion, and that brought tears flooding from my eyes. I began to tell the girls of my (at that time) seventy-plus days of a migraine and how He provides daily God winks to let me know He is still in control and I should trust Him. Many, many of these days I've been weary and I've questioned His plan, and that small rock with such a powerful word was that day's God wink for sure.

- I am captivated by old churches, steeples, and bridges. I love to stop and capture pictures of these when I see them. David knows these things truly make me happy, and he occasionally finds them, captures their picture, and sends them to me, knowing it'll make me smile. He knows the things I love, and they are special to both of us. The fact that God brought me a soul mate that will do this for me makes both my heart and face smile with unbelief and gratefulness. (Update: Marcy, one of my daughters-in-law, has started doing the exact same thing! Marcy goes on business trips and sends me the most beautiful

"Shelley pictures" that I could ever ask for. God sends His grace through sweet Marcy.)

❤

Thank You for Your small, subtle confirmations.

From my heart to yours:

Begin now looking for the God winks in your life and jot them down, share them, and encourage others to do the same:

My prayer for you:

Lord, what amazing things You show us if we will just look for them. Help us today to look for You in everything, and help us to find the God winks along our journeys. Lord, I pray we never forget the greatness of who You are.

His healing words to your heart:

"No one is like you, Lord; you are great, and your name is mighty in power" (Jeremiah 10:6).

Chapter 28:
Hope and Strength

Lord I crawled across the barrenness to You with my empty cup uncertain asking any small drop of refreshment. If only I had known You better I'd have come running with a bucket. —*Nancy Spiegelberg*

I love those words.

How many times do we expect Him to provide a drop and He fills buckets for us? What He provides, way exceeds our expectations for Him. Hope is a gentle kiss to the fingertips, blown softly away that sends faith softly rising.

He is still pouring! Just when you think your hope has slipped, He will come through for you. He has to bring us to our weakest point to make us strong. Let hope anchor your soul.

Oftentimes we awake with the gloom and doom of the previous night in our minds, carrying it to the following day, stealing joy from the day that God has provided us. So try to teach yourself that no matter what happened the day before, this is the day He has provided. Don't let it go in haste. Try to capture joy. If we all tried a little harder each day to make this world a better place, I bet we would succeed. Try and honor Him with every breath.

I am thankful that every morning, without fail, no matter what challenges I have been through the previous night, God allows for the clouds to part, as if a velvet curtain on a stage, to unveil His vivid canvas-inspired sun to rise, each brushstroke having its own character and individuality, while birds sing as if they were excited children in their very first Christmas program.

God is everywhere we go; before we get there, He's already prepared our path. Nothing that happens surprises Him. He never says, "Oh, wow, didn't see that coming" as we often do.

Your sun will never set again, and your moon will wane no more; the Lord will be your everlasting light, and your days of sorrow will end. —Isaiah 60:20

We let the stress of this world consume us and sometimes destroy us. All the while, He's waiting on us to believe that He can come through for us. He may put a "giant" in front of you so you can see how strong you really are. Where our strength ends, His Will begins.

I keep my eyes always on the Lord. With him at my right hand, I will not be shaken. —Psalm 16:8

There are things in our lives that we don't even know we need until we have them and realize we were starving for that very thing (trust, love, strength, and knowing we matter). Once we get one of these, we typically can't get enough.

Sometimes you may feel as if life should stop when things get so complicated; however, life continues. The sun rises and sets, and the moon and the stars still sparkle in the night, even in our darkest hours, and weeds still grow between the cracks in our driveways. Life continues and so shall we. It's all perspective, or our perception of how we see things. What filter or lens do you look through? One of hope, gratitude, or maybe anger? Clean or clear your lens today, it'll change your tomorrow. I always wanted good to triumph over evil—and it did, it does, it will!

I am feeling very blessed at where I am when I turn around and see how far I've come. I remember walking the path as if barefoot in a field of mesquite trees, trying to reach the green meadow while stopping to pick out thorns from my feet along the way, all the while wondering if I could make it.

"When you pass through the waters, I will be with you; and when you pass through the rivers, they will not sweep over you. When you walk through the fire, you will not be burned; the flames will not set you ablaze." —Isaiah 43:2

Today I *dance* in the meadow!

There's irony in being told you *can't* do something, or you're not good enough, then being your best at it. I remember when I didn't believe in myself, but He provided the strength for me to believe in Him, and that was all I needed. And it's all you need!

Whether you are on top of a mountain, arms flailing with joy, deep in a valley of stillness, or in a canyon that is widening with every breath, never forget where you've come from or where you've been. Look back occasionally just to see how far you've come and never be afraid to return to the well. Life gets hard every now and then, even during times of plenty and great blessings.

> *He gives strength to the weary and increases*
> *the power of the weak. —Isaiah 40:29*

I am a new person—stronger, bolder—or maybe I'm who I always was and just didn't realize it, or that "me" had been crushed for far too long. I will never, ever let anyone take advantage of me again. By God's grace and with His help, I have strength, I am strong. My heart beats again.

I wanted to stand tall after all my inequities, and I am—I am stronger than I've ever been. God is using my life now as a witness, a form of daily encouragement, strength, and hope to so many. My life is a picture of what He can do if you let Him. So many people watched me go through the fire and come out the other side, and I hope they gained strength and renewed their trust in Him along the way. If what I went through helps to change someone's life, it will have all been worth it. He helped me "walk this out." He can help you too. You just have to let Him.

"But those who wait on the Lord Shall renew their strength; they shall mount up with wings like eagles, they shall run and not grow weary, they shall walk and not faint" (Isaiah 40:31 NKJV). Little did I know, all those years as a child, with Nanny, hearing her quote this scripture that it would come to mean so much to me. Who knew? He did, all the while!

> *Cast your cares on the Lord and he will sustain you; he will*
> *never let the righteous be shaken. —Psalm 55:22*

To rise fully, I had to fall to my knees. Well, what if you don't want to stand, you don't have the strength to stand, or you just want to sit with your head between your legs and weep? Bravery doesn't always mean standing. Sometimes the bravest thing to do is to sit and breathe, and when you're ready to take that step, He'll already be there waiting. When you feel like you've fallen, He's moved you right to where He wants you to be.

You can change or stay the same, there are no rules to this thing. We can make the best or worst of it. I hope you make the best of it, and I hope you see things that startle you. I hope you feel things you never felt before. I hope you meet people with a different point of view. I hope you have the strength to start all over again. —F. Scott Fitzgerald

Psalm 23 actually speaks of *movement* to me: passing through, moving through, and getting through—conquering the Promised Land. Maybe for you that means your toughest time in life. Verses 2–3 say, "He makes me lie down in green pastures, he leads me beside quiet waters, he refreshes my soul." I love to see it as life and living. I love using this psalm as encouragement to conquer through.

And even though it all went wrong, I'll stand before the Lord of song with nothing on my tongue but Hallelujah. —Leonard Cohen

Sometimes our hallelujahs are broken, but give Him the praise and honor with whatever breath you have. Our "wrong" is His "right." What you are going through is exactly what He means for you. While the room is dark, dreary, and dim; look for His light. Look for His blessings, no matter how small, even in your darkest hours. He knows you are broken. Let Him use you. Let Him walk this out with you, and then, forever sing His praises!

❤

A million thank-yous, Lord. Truly, I can never thank You enough! You believed in me during times when I couldn't even

*believe in myself. For it's by my weakness
that You made me strong.*

From my heart to yours:

- What do you hope for?

- Can you put your faith in motion?

- How often are you *thankful*? Are you *intentionally* thankful and live thankfully with every breath?

- Take a moment and list some things you are thankful for, or if you can't list several, list just one.

My prayer for you:

Lord, we pray and believe, truly, that where our strength ends is where Your will begins. When we walk broken through the thorns of the mesquite trees, provide us breath and hope to keep walking. Whether we sing hallelujahs or barely utter a breath, may we know Your love for us is boundless.

His healing words to your heart:

"In all this you greatly rejoice, though now for a little while you may have had to suffer grief in all kinds of trials. These have come so that the proven genuineness of your faith—of greater worth than gold, which perishes even though refined by fire—may result in praise, glory and honor when Jesus Christ is revealed" (1 Peter 1:6–7).

Chapter 29:

The Beauty of Mercy and Grace

Hear my prayer, Lord;
listen to my cry for mercy. —Psalm 86:6

Once again, I am so humbled by His grace! I can't tell you how many days this has happened in this new life of mine. On many occasions, I have laid in bed, pondering the beauty of His mercy and grace that He bestows on us and that He has bestowed on me.

Take for instance the years that were woven with pain, sadness, and countless tears; I can't tell you how many prayers I prayed for God to provide His healing or provide me a way to my heart's safety. He provided!

Did I believe that would happen? Not truly, for many years! I kept getting in the way of His blessing, His answered prayer. His grace! I pray that story of His great blessing will indeed be another writing someday when I have more time to give it the proper words that it deserves!

His mercy is what allows us to escape, gain strength, and make it through! His grace is where the blessings came from, and so many times He provided mercifully for me. God graciously showed His mercy on Mother, and at the same time He was there for us, her children, His children. Every time my mother was absent from my life, He was there. He never left me! He was there molding me into who I am today.

As far back as I can remember, He has poured His grace on me. When the dark veil of my mother's drugs and alcohol covered us in darkness, His mercy allowed us girls to "unwrap" the darkness, the sin, the filth, the shame and begin again, walking with Him in His grace and light. His grace is amazing!

So all of us who have had that veil removed can see and reflect the glory of the Lord. And the Lord—who is the Spirit—makes us more and more like him as we are changed into his glorious image. —2 Corinthians 3:18 NLT

Mother sipped vodka, and we took a "sip of life." The difference is incomprehensible.

Why did she not see life as we did?
What was life to her?
Why were we "thirsty" for such different things?
Why couldn't she have a thirst for things that mattered?

Mother saw life literally through a half-empty glass or a tipped-over pill bottle. We lived a life of "bottles of abandonment" at times. Her life must have been a blur or a complete fog. I love to see life vibrant and clear, and quite frankly I hate the feeling you get from taking medicine.

Life with Him is amazing. He will meet you where you are. Whether you're full or empty, thirsty or quenched, bring Him what you have, and bring Him what you are. Who you are and what you have is fine with Him.

I understand a little better now that it wasn't His "grace," but rather His mercy, that allowed us to survive. And it is His grace that we continue to live in so wonderfully!

One night at David's, before we were married, Nanny (David's mom) came in from Deer Park to visit. I had the honor of sitting and watching generations play, laugh, and love in such a simple setting—David's living room. I have always been a "simple" girl, loving the simple things in life, the things you can't buy but have a worth beyond belief! Nanny gripped my heart and reminded me so much of my Mammaw. When I saw this jewel, I realized how God had sprinkled these women all over our planet to provide His blessings in so many deserving places and how often I had been a recipient.

My Mammaw was a true woman of God who touched so many lives during hers. Kimberley always said she wanted to be just like her, a true Jesus lover and follower and through God's amazing grace, she is. God used this special woman that night as not only a reminder to me of those wonderful qualities that have been passed down through the generations, but as a reminder of His goodness to us!

I am so magnificently grateful for who He has provided, how He has provided, and that He continues to provide for Taylor and me! Some mornings I open my eyes and say out loud, "Is this my life?" With tears streaming down my face, I answer myself. Let me be the first to tell you I have had His grace poured on me, but right now it is raining grace! It is everywhere I look, everywhere I go, everywhere I breathe. Now, anyone who knows me knows that I scoop up the grace, then put it in bottles and buckets as fast as I can for those who I might encounter who need some as well.

❤

May today be a true blessing to many, a raining of Your sweet grace. Let us dance in the rain!

From my heart to yours:

- How do you see mercy and grace? How has He provided you with both?

- What blessings has He poured on you?

- Do you dance in the rain?

My prayer for you:

I pray with everything in me that His grace will fall like rain on everyone who has blessed me with reading these words. I am overcome with gratefulness. May every morning bring a new raining of His sweet, sweet grace and may His mercy leave you breathless. Jesus, bring the rain; may it be an all-out downpour where no umbrellas are needed.

His healing words to your heart:

"Because of the Lord's great love we are not consumed, for his compassions never fail" (Lamentations 3:22–23).

Chapter 30:
Be Still and Know He is God

God is our refuge and strength, an ever-present
help in trouble. Therefore we will not fear,
though the earth give way and the mountains fall into
the heart of the sea, though its waters roar and foam and
the mountains quake with their surging. —Psalm 46:1

When asked by a dear friend to do the Vision Walk one year, Taylor and I eagerly said yes as my grandmother (Nanny) had Macular Degeneration, and I lived watching her struggle on many occasions. The Vision Walk raises money for the Foundation Fighting Blindness to fund research for eye diseases such as Retinitis Pigmentosa, Macular Degeneration, Usher Syndrome, and a multitude of other retinal degenerative diseases. Another connection to the Vision Walk is that Taylor has Irlen Syndrome, along with her Dyslexia, which makes her so sensitive to light, eye strain, etc.[3]

I never dreamed that I would be poisoned and struggle

daily with vision issues myself (light sensitivity, blurriness, night vision glare, computer glare, film covering my eyes late at night, nausea and anxiety when reading, headaches, poor depth perception, and trouble telling colors).

For we live by faith, not by sight. —2 Corinthians 5:7

Well, we woke up the morning of the walk seeing it rain (we immediately began looking for ponchos, umbrellas, etc. to take to the walk) and never ever did it cross our minds not to go. We wouldn't let a little rain stop us; we had people to help. We had worked so hard "selling our carrots." Taylor and I tried to think of a creative way to collect money for the walk, and we decided that since carrots are good for your eyes, and this walk definitely was about the eyes, that we would go to the store and buy "real" carrots (long green leaves and every-thing) and sell them. It was easier to ask people to "buy a car-rot" instead of just asking them to make a donation. So many donated (and no one took their carrots by the way). We sold the same carrots over and over. What fun! This was one of those times when we just had to think out of the box.

One thing I noticed about the morning was that Taylor did not take her purple Irlen syndrome glasses, and had the sun been out, she would have had no choice but to wear her "purple glasses" or wear her nonprescription dark sunglasses to combat the sun's glare. But, since it was raining and she walked out without her glasses, I began thinking that had it been a bright, beaming, sunny day what havoc it would have wreaked on so many eyes, including hers, at the walk. Remember, the eyes were why we were there. *Is God in con-*

---

3 Meares-Irlen syndrome, scotopic sensitivity syndrome, and visual stress is a perceptual processing disorder. It is not an optical problem. It is a problem with the brain's ability to process visual information (see www.Irlen.com).

trol? Absolutely! He can adjust the easiest and most complex things in this world of ours, and we were so grateful for the clouds that morning.

Another point I realized was that even with all the people doing the walk, I walked 99 percent of the walk by myself. I had three miles of prayer and meditation while smelling the rain, feeling the rain, seeing everything burst green from the fresh rain, watching the ducks, and seeing the spider cling to the web as the rain made it so unstable.

I walked almost one and a half miles behind a girl who appeared to be about my age walking with her dad (I would guess) and her service dog. I noticed the dog never missed a step through every puddle. It was clear that this dog knew his job and knew this girl depended on him. Rain would not change his ways. I fought back tears many, many times. And many times the tears won. God is so good!

Show us Your *glory*.

Rain or shine He's always there, in every situation, good or bad. If we will only ask Him, He will show us the glory we seek. We often just "notice" Him when we see Him in a rainbow, a storm, nature, a hillside or meadow, a bird singing, a beautiful countryside, or a spider web, but He is also in the tears that fall from grieving faces, and I encourage you to be still and know that He is God!

> *"The Lord will fight for you;*
> *you need only to be still." —Exodus 14:14*

❤

Lord, thank You for showing me how to just be still. Help us just to know the true depth of who You are, and be quiet enough to listen. I thank You for that day and all its blessings, and I ask that You continue to bless all the eyes we helped that day. You are in so many things that we pass by and take for granted. Help us to see You.

From my heart to yours:

- Name some places or things that you see God in. How can you be still and just know?

- What keeps you from being still?

My prayer for you:

Lord, help us to be still and let the magnitude of who You are sink in. Lord, calm whatever keeps us from resting in Your presence. I pray you will breathe Him in and lean into His Majesty. Lord, help us to see Your glory with more than just our eyes. Oh, how we love You.

His healing words to your heart:

"Now then, stand still and see this great thing the Lord is about to do before your eyes!" (1 Samuel 12:16).

Chapter 31:
Memories and the Lack Thereof

*Praise be to the God and Father of our Lord Jesus Christ, the
Father of compassion and the God of all comfort, who com-
forts us in all our troubles, so that we can comfort those in
any trouble with the comfort we ourselves receive from God.*
—2 Corinthians 1:3-4

Over the years, I've recognized that post brain injury I've
become an introvert. This realization was hard for me knowing I had spent approximately 46 years as an extrovert. Noise
to me now is horribly stressful, and once I told David that I
used to be the one making the noise. Quiet now is a godsend
and when presented is usually much needed. One of the hardest things I've had to learn to do is listen to my brain. When it
says "enough," it's definitely enough. When it says "rest," rest is
probably long overdue. It's hard, real hard. I've voiced numerous times that somedays I use so much brain activity that my
goal is to end the day with just enough brain cells to be able to

drive the car home.

This is reality somedays, and these are the days that I try to extend myself grace, or I curl up in a pool of tears—sometimes both.

I've also realized that so many memories that I have are surrounded by a quarter-inch white square frame (photograph). This, by far, is one of the hardest things I've had to realize and accept, and this is why so many times my response is, "Did we have fun?" My memories are most commonly pictures that I've seen over the years, pictures taken with either a Kodak Instamatic or Polaroid camera, and now by someone's nearby cell phone trying to bring back a memory. You never know just how important a picture will become until you are tasked with remembering something that is forever gone.

I know how beautiful my niece Misty was at her wedding by the stunning wedding portrait of her that hangs in my sister Kimberley's bedroom. I know I was there and what I wore by the 8x10 family portrait that I've seen many times. I know how cute Taylor was as a flower girl and that her hair was adorned with bobby pins and hairspray. In my head, I can see around her in the picture a mixture of big girls, little girls, blonde curls, braids, curling irons, hairspray bottles, bobby pins, brushes, rattail combs, and such. Beauty in the making.

Pictures are worth a thousand words or one memory. You never know when in the blink of an eye or the inhale of your next breath, they may be gone! Memories leave as if fire set to a string. I never dreamed this would've happened to me. So many things that we take for granted. *You may not always remember.* In the beginning, it seems easy and so far removed from where you are right now, but it may just become a reality. I pray it doesn't! I pray no one should ever experience this; it's frustrating and on many days frightening.

Courtney remembers a lot of memories of not only our

Shelley Taylor

life, but of me. A few years ago, she gave me one of the most thoughtful gifts I had ever received. She gave me a precious notebook where she recorded memories of me! She wrote on the first few pages, and there are plenty left for me to record memories remembered or current events that will soon be memories that may stay or may be forever forgotten. When you have difficulty remembering and someone provides you detailed memories that have escaped you forever, words can't express the impact this made. The very worst thing someone with a brain injury can do is to say, *"I'll remember this"* or *"I don't need to write this down."* Courtney, I love you!

Here is Courtney's favorite memory of Mother:

> *We were in church at Acton United Methodist, and it was around 1974. I remember singing and looking over at Mother standing close beside me. Mother gave me the most beautiful smile, full of Love and pride! I smiled back and we just stood there a moment, smiling at each other. It was the most intimate moment I ever shared with my mother, and the one I cherish above all others.*

I share this with you as it's such a sweet memory of who Mother *was*.

❤

Each memory and picture is a reminder that You brought us through. Lord, never quit reminding us.

From my heart to yours:

- What memories bring you (strength, hope, joy, comfort)?

- What memories bring you (weakness, despair, sorrow, pain)?

- What new memories can you begin making today? Write down as many memories as you can. (write in the mar-

204

gins or make a memory journal) Trust me, you'll wish you had, if the moment comes that they are gone. Next time you need a gift idea, gift someone with their own memory journal.

My prayer for you:

Lord, I pray that moment never comes for them, that in an inhale of a breath their memories are lost forever. Help us all to extend ourselves grace when needed and know it's perfectly fine to curl up in a pool of tears.

His healing words to your heart:

"Let us then approach God's throne of grace with confidence, so that we may receive mercy and find grace to help us in our time of need" (Hebrews 4:16).

Chapter 32:
Death and Life Thereafter

"Blessed are those who mourn, for they will be comforted."
—Matthew 5:4

God's ultimate showing of grace was during the breaths we took when our parents were dying. His Hand gently surrounded us and brought our family together. Sometimes we try to plan out our next breath, or our next steps, only to have Him put a turn in the road, a wiggle, or a stop sign. Sometimes the road is deeply winding and we feel overcome by what we're presented with. This was us. This was a time when we had to lace up our boot straps and walk because people were depending on us; Dadi depended on us for his and Mother's breaths. We had to walk even if we stumbled while drips of hope were shed. This was a time when we all at one point or another were both leaders and limpers on any given day. Every day presented new challenges. Whoever had enough breath to face what was facing us took charge.

God brought us hard, but in the end, His *love* didn't fail.

Of all the choices Mother made during her life, the choice she made December 1, 2014, would prove to be the *fatal choice*. While our dad lay in the hospital with a 90 percent clogged artery, our mom, at home, reached for the drugs that Dadi had intentionally moved out of her reach. She fell, sustaining a broken neck and a fatal blow to the head. When the paramedics called to let me know what had happened and that they were taking her to Harris downtown, my immediate response was, "You have to take her to Mansfield Methodist. That's where my dad is!" They quickly told me she had sustained a life-threatening injury that would require the trauma unit at Harris. While he was still speaking, I told them I was on my way and hung up before even hearing their response.

Each breath she took brought her a little closer to her last.

Not long after Taylor and I arrived, we were told that Mother's injuries would indeed take her life. I was both numb and angry for her selfish choice and incredibly sad for what Dadi didn't know yet and for all the breaths he had invested in her. Dadi had shown her unconditional love for over fifty years, and she continued to put herself and her addiction first. Taylor made a multitude of phone calls to people she knew at Mansfield Methodist to try and expedite Dadi's treatment as we knew we had to get Dadi to Mother as quickly as we could.

My husband, David, went and temporarily checked Dadi out so he could come tell his wife good-bye. David told him that Mother had fallen, but not that she wouldn't make it. They drove twenty miles to Harris Hospital in downtown Fort Worth, making small talk while David's heart was being seared by the secret it held. I continually prayed while they drove for both Dadi and David's hearts. I met them at the street, pushed Dadi in a wheelchair to Mother's room, and spoke some of the hardest words I've ever spoken while my hands trembled and lips quivered. "Dadi, she's not gonna make it this time."

This was a time in my life when I had "expected" something so many times and it never came. Then when it did, I didn't expect it. This was truly God's timing and His plan.

Forty years of longing for a mother was finally in its last chapter, its last verse, so to speak. I was sitting in the hospice ward watching Mother struggle to breathe her last breaths. With each breath she breathed, I wondered if that would be her last. I pondered on all the breaths that she had linked together in her seventy-five years.

Peace is the journey of a thousand miles, and it must be taken one step at a time. —Lyndon B. Johnson

That last night, while sitting by her side, I thought of no longer hearing her voice. The irony was, she and I never sat and shared beautiful words, but the sadness that her voice would be gone forever. Mentally Mother left us so many years ago due to all the abuse to her body.

Even if Mother sat in front of me at that moment, the chance to find out if I were truly a twin couldn't have presented itself. The reality was setting in that her breaths were narrowing, and the chance to even know the truth was closing. Then Mother drew her last breath, taking with her the truth of something so significant, so sacred to me, yet not worthy of spoken words all these years. *Why was something so important to me not important to her?*

There was the most beautiful angel that was brightly lit that hung outside our mother's room while she faded. In our darkest hour, this angel lit the night while our hope sank, tears were flooding, as well as God's grace.

The following are some things we wrote along the way while we savored Dadi's last moments:

December 2014 our worlds changed. We will savor the moments and trust Him for our dad's remaining breaths and heartbeats. Our mom fell, suffered a fatal traumatic brain injury and passed away December 5th. Four days later (on his birthday no doubt) our dad suffered a massive stroke and every type of language that we have is deeply compromised and he has great difficulty speaking and communicating. Normally one would be challenged in a specific area of language, but for Dadi it's all of them. He's able to lift his right arm and leg, but cannot feel them, unable to walk or hold a pen. Humming is therapeutic for him and has been his best form of therapy and so we may just sing and hum him through the remainder of his journey. The medicine that was given to reverse some of the damage (could help up to 30 percent) came with great risks of bleeding and death. It was confirmed at 1:00 a.m. this morning that he does indeed have a brain bleed from the medicine. They will continue to monitor the bleed and if it becomes stable then he will go to a stroke rehab for up to 2 months. If it continues to grow larger, then his outcome is grim. Surgery for his 90 percent blocked carotid artery (which is the appointment he was going to when this happened) is temporarily off the table, so the possibility of future strokes still remains. The neurologist asked us not to mention Mother's death as it would be too traumatic for Dadi's brain injury.

This was written to my coworkers, who hugged me, prayed with me and for me, cried with me, wiped my tears, and listened to me the week after our mom died and just days after our dad suffered a massive stroke four days after her death.

Words normally do not escape me. While most of you know that I do find great comfort in writing and writing out my journey in this life, right now I am at a loss for words. Last week I wrote the following at my mother's dying side, "No words." I believe someday soon I will be able to write this journey out, but for now it is all too unsure and constantly changing. Eventually we will have a small memorial for Mother with immediate family, but our concern is to get Dadi better first. God had different plans than ours and now we are following His lead and asking Him to direct our paths with Dadi. There is a possibility that the bleed will not stop and then we will have the memorial for both of them. Meanwhile, my mom's body is still at the Medical Examiners although they have finished with her. We are waiting on Dadi's discharge paperwork from his service years ago in the Army before they can go and pick up her body. Too many things are uncertain right now and we have no other choice but to trust Him. I pray my faith will not waiver, but for now I totally trust Him and will just watch for little God Winks along the way. I cannot begin to express my sincere love for you all and truly thank you all for loving me through this. oxox, Shelley"

Dadi finally asked about Mother:

Tuesday, January 13, 2015

Just had a long talk with Dadi, mostly me talking. He started with "Where?" We ended up talking about Mother. I told him she was cremated and was at Courtney's safe and sound. He said, "Yay!" I told him that the plan was to wait and do a memorial when he could be there and that eventually their ashes would be comingled together and placed at the National Cemetery. He said, "Good, good." I also let him know we were told not to mention Mother until he did because it would be too hard on him to try and talk, etc. I said, "I guess you wanted to let us know you knew when Reese (Kimberley's oldest daughter,

Misty's oldest daughter) came." He said, "Yes!" We both cried a little. I said, "It's sad" and he said, "Yes." Then he was ok. He's eating lunch now and is just fine, and there's nothing about me that is.

He *heals* the brokenhearted and
binds up their wounds. —Psalm 147:3

This was from Kim's heart to her friends that she knew were praying:

Tuesday, January 20, 2015

Hey Ladies, please forgive the long wait for an update. We didn't get my dad moved until last Wednesday. He was approved on Tuesday night at 6:00 and we didn't leave the rehab until 5:00 on Wednesday. Good thing is, he was able to have therapy that day. He hadn't had therapy for 5 days at that point (his case worker let him fall through the cracks). I arrived at the nursing home ahead of him and met my sister Shelley and niece Taylor there. We waited for him and then started paperwork, etc. Taylor and I took her truck to their house and I completely lost it! I knew leaving my dad there was going to be one of the hardest things I had ever done in my life, and it was! We made sure all was in order and as it should be at the nursing home before Shelley, Taylor, and I went to dinner. I cried when I left the nursing home and walking into the restaurant again, twice while we ate and then I bawled all the way to my mom and dad's apartment.

Needless to say, none of us got a lot of sleep that night, including my dad. There was adjusting the next couple of days, for all of us. The people at the nursing home are very kind, compassionate, loving people but let's just face it, it's still a nursing home. We have decorated his room, brought his TV, moved his bed to the window, and even got him a bird feeder to hang on the tree outside his window to make things a bit better. He got there Wednesday night and earlier in the week my daughter Charlsey suggested we go to dinner and a movie. So, Thursday night Shelley came by to check on Daddy after work around 4:30 when I left, and Charlsey and I went with Taylor and her boyfriend, Keifer, to dinner and a movie to pretend things were somewhat normal.

In the middle of the movie, Shelley sent a text (around 9:00) that my dad had fallen. He wasn't hurt badly, a scrape to his arm, but come on people this is still just the second day. Needless to say, I had several conversations with staff the following day before I headed home for some much-needed rest. I'm getting much-needed things done at home (I can't stop being busy), which is my stress reliever. I'll head back to finish packing and move everything out the week of the 26th.

This all still seems as though none of it has really happened and I'm living someone else's life right now, but God is still on His throne and His mercies are truly new every morning! I am so grateful to have Him as my strength daily and for all of you beside me on this journey. If God so desires, Billy and I would love for my dad to come and live with us. There are many roads to travel before then, but this is my prayer! I'm also praying daily for all of you! Know you are loved and missed daily. Thanks for your support.

In Him and For Him,

Kimberley Tye

Tuesday, January 20, 2015

Dadi is doing well, but it will be a long road. When I was leaving him this morning, we saw a man walking on a walker and I told him, "That will be you someday." He said, "Yep, yep." Then, as he struggled greatly to tell me something, I told him the words will come and he said, "One day." I've heard Dadi say "yep," "nope," "ok," "I will," "one day," "right," "stop," and "I love you." "I love you" broke my heart! The people are very, very kind, but Kim's words are true: it is still a nursing home. He does love the fellowship with others (even if he struggles) that he missed for so many years taking care of Mother. We can't thank you all enough for your prayers through this journey; we wouldn't want to walk it without you!

Agonizing days continued, ministrokes continued until the final stroke the day of Mother and Dadi's wedding anniversary the end of March. We heard the words we knew were coming but didn't want to hear, which led us to the familiar hospice facility where Mother had her final breath.

Watching Dadi fade was painful. Listening to his breath failing was agonizing, and I hoped each breath would be his last and his pain would end. So many people have experienced the same thing with their loved ones, and if that's you, I'm sorry. During those last moments, I felt as if my peace was both *gone* and *granted* all at the same time. Grief is piercing, and then grace shows up. Grief is different for all of us and none of us know how deep each other's grief is. Some people are not even pierced by grief, and with others it leaves an ugly gaping hole.

"He will wipe every tear from their eyes. There will be no more death or mourning or crying or pain, for the old order of things has passed away." —Revelation 21:4

*Grief is the last act of Love that we can show
to those we have loved and lost. —Unknown*

We slept on cots, couches, windowsills and didn't sleep as well, all the while watching and listening to the clock tick and our parents breathe. Both loving and losing affect each other deep and some deeper.

Both horrible words and beautiful prayers came from our mouths while sitting at hospice. We spoke love and anger, hugged and hated from the same lips to each other and God. Emotions were out of control.

Loss or grief connects us with those left, those who we suffer with, and no two people grieve the same. And one things for certain, grief often catches you unaware.

Even a year later, grief caught me off guard in what was supposed to be a time of joy. Has this ever happened to you? I was overcome with the emotion that it was Christmas-time, and for many people, I knew that the feeling of joy just doesn't come. This time of year, you can't not hear "Joy to the World." It resonates everywhere we go.

I wrote the following on my blog as my Mother had died the prior December, and the anniversary of her death brought deep emotion. My sister Courtney was heavy on my heart as I know her grief is paralyzing, and my heart was breaking for her and for those who are joyless.

What happens when joy doesn't come in the morning?

- *What happens when joy doesn't fill your soul?*
- *What happens when everyone has joy but you?*

I just returned from the DFW Cemetery, where both of my parents' ashes are comingled. Their place of rest looks out over the most incredible sunsets and oftentimes when we are there our sadness is comingled with these incredible sunsets as well. Tonight, we took a dozen lavender roses to honor Mother and her death. It is always a rough week on my family.

My mother died (on a Friday night). The following Tuesday morning I was at work, talking with a coworker about all the events with my mom and I had literally just spoken the words, "But joy comes in the morning" when my eldest sister called and stated that my dad was in the car with her in the process of having a stroke. He indeed suffered a massive stroke that would change his and our lives forever. Our lives had just been changed four days earlier and just when you think you can't change anymore, God oftentimes has a different plan. I hope I never forget that I stated, "But joy comes in the morning" that day as it truly does if we allow it to. Sometimes joy has to be intentional, but my heart aches for those who physically can't make that happen for one reason or another.

❤

Lord, I pray for peace, comfort, and mercy for those who need You just a little extra this time of year. Those who need an extra measure of grace or just need You to nestle in a little closer right now. I thank You that I am joyful and my hope is bright because I know it was only by my trusting You that You saw me through and continue to see me through each and every day. Lord, thank You for life, thank You for saving my and Taylor's lives, and thank You for all my family, near and far, and most importantly for the birth of Jesus! May we celebrate Him in whatever way we can whether our joy fills a teaspoon or fills a bucket. Shine Your light on us and through us in this darkened world. May your joy come in the morning!

From my heart to yours:
- Share your feelings of grief: shock and denial, pain and guilt, (guilt if you were left and they died), anger, (angry

at the person for dying), (angry at God for taking them), depression and sadness, acceptance, relief, hope.

• What is something you have *longed for, loved, and lost?*

My prayer for you:

Thank You for coming through when we needed You so desperately. Our worlds were crumbling with grief, and You provided an extra measure of grace when we so frantically needed it. Even when we are so weak we stumble, or our joy doesn't come, He is there picking up our tears, and I pray you have enough breath to face what He puts in your path. I pray God covers you in His grace and mercy the next time you grieve, and you feel His Hand of mercy.

His healing words to your heart:

"The Lord is close to the brokenhearted and saves those who are crushed in spirit" (Psalm 34:18).

Chapter 33:
Cradle to Cross

Many are the plans in a person's heart, but it is the Lord's
purpose that prevails. —Proverbs 19:21

Holly (one of my bonus daughters) has a passion for single
pregnant girls, and she told me one day that it was her heart's
desire to start an Embrace Grace group (embracegrace.com)
at our church, Walnut Ridge Baptist Church. (It's a ministry
for single girls who find themselves in an unplanned pregnancy.) She asked me if I'd like to be a leader, and I gladly
said yes. Through most of the semesters, Taylor has helped as
well, and it's become a special part of our lives, us making a
difference in their lives and them making a difference in ours.

Recently, Taylor, my sister Kimberley, and I were at a Pink
Impact Women's Conference through Gateway Church and
were able to witness firsthand one of Embrace Grace's found-
ers, Amy Ford, speak about her life and this beautiful ministry. Amy spoke, we listened, and women were changed!

Hearts were changed that day, and the Embrace Grace booth was flooded with women who either needed to be engulfed in grace or wanted to embrace grace on others. Out of the 10,000 plus women, it's safe to say that most women either knew someone who had an unexpected pregnancy, had one themselves, or had their heart touched enough to want to be there for someone who hasn't seen the positive sign on a pregnancy test yet, or someone who already has. God was amongst us that day.

The purpose of Embrace Grace is to show these girls "Blooms"—God's incredible *grace*— and wrap them gently in it.

We, as Christians who are pro-life, encourage single pregnant girls to keep their babies. We want them to either raise them or place them for adoption. As a society, when we see a single pregnant girl, we "shun" her—the same girls that we encouraged to stay pregnant. We stop short of offering discipleship and nurturing them. The beauty of Embrace Grace is it engulfs them into love, self-worth, hope, grace, trust, and faith that He will see them through. We bring the church to the "Bloom" and offer it as their *first* resort, instead of their *last*. It's also a great ministry to the church itself. Sometimes God puts what we preach into physical bodies with breath to help us practice what we preach. And sometimes this is amazing, and this is one of those times!

No matter where you are in your life, don't you need to *embrace grace?*

Sometimes we just need to embrace ourselves in His grace, and sometimes we just need to embrace others with it. This ministry has changed my life and the lives of two of my daughters, and it thrills me to walk this journey out with both Holly and Taylor! We have connected and created life-long friendships with the other leaders that we serve with and all those who began Embrace Grace, and it's been life-changing. I have witnessed God's Hand being placed on a ministry and reassuring us over and over that this is His Will. It's an awesome feeling to stand hand in hand with your daughters while they grasp hands of terrified girls who desperately need someone to help their faith conquer their fear. God has smiled on these girls and brought them all closer to Him, and in this process, He brought us closer to Him as well. We, as leaders, set out to bless these girls and have found ourselves drowning in the outpouring of grace and mercy He has bestowed on us through their sweet lives. It is not we who have blessed them; it is *God*.

One night, one of the "Blooms" said she felt as if she were a piece of a beautiful puzzle. She is, isn't she? We all are. He made us beautiful; each of us having our own part in His plan. We've seen many Blooms become leaders in either Embrace Grace or Embrace Life. (Embrace Life is for single moms, and typically is where the Blooms go after Embrace Grace, and our church offers both.) This ministry truly is life changing for all involved!

Kimberley always says, "As long as He has us here, there is His work to do." She's right. Remember it's all about Him. In such a short time, we have seen these "Blooms" grow so much, their lives forever changed. They have made forever friends and forever family with us as leaders. And we have had the honor of praying for them, clothing them in His sweet, sweet grace, and bringing them closer to the cross.

The funny thing is that when they get there, they'll see us

too, one hand extended back to them and the other extended up towards Him. We are all just stumbling towards Jesus.

God's work comes with almost daily blows from the devil, but we serve an almighty God, a conqueror, and He has taught us to be conquerors as well. And we are changing lives two heartbeats at a time. Satan has brought sickness, migraines, cancer, busyness, car wrecks, death and power outages to try and stop God's work, but if you have to wrap shower presents via candlelight and no air conditioning, that's what you do.

What *brings* you to the cross?

I have told the "Blooms," it is unfortunate for them that they "wear" their sin on their bellies for the entire world to see. What if we all had to write our sin with Sharpies all over us, for the world to view? People easily place blame when their sins are hidden. What if we just extended more of His love? It is our responsibility as Christians to do His work and share His saving grace; shouldn't we start at the cradle and end at the cross?

❤

Lord, I pray we would envelop single pregnant moms, supporting them and ministering to them and that precious beating heart inside. Let us see them with Your eyes.

From my heart to yours:
- If you see a single pregnant girl, do you show her God's grace or shun her?
- Who can you bring closer to the cross by showing them God's incredible grace (maybe you could start an Embrace Grace at your church)?

My prayer for you:

Lord, I pray we become vessels to extend grace as You've extended grace to us. How often are we not worthy, but You never stop pouring on us. Bring us those who need You and let us wrap them in Your love. Thank You for embracing us in your sweet grace.

His healing words to your heart:

"Each of you should use whatever gift you have received to serve others, as faithful stewards of God's grace in its various forms" (1 Peter 4:10).

Chapter 34:
Fire Pits, our Faith, and His Faithfulness

From the ends of the earth I call to you,
I call as my heart grows faint; Lead me to the rock
that is higher than I. —Psalm 61:2

This is Kinsley's story, as told by Tara, her sweet mama (our daughter-in-law). Kinsley is the precious little girl on the cover of this book, our only granddaughter out of eight grandchildren. She was three at the time of this event. This was the morning our hearts beat in overtime and our breaths halted.

On the morning of November 27, 2016, our daughter, Kinsley, fell into the hot ashes of the fire pit at our ranch (TTT Ranch) in Cisco, Texas. This was the scariest moment of our lives!

We woke up that morning and fixed breakfast while the kids were playing around camp. Kinsley was playing with her brother and cousin. After breakfast, we all started cleaning up to go home. I was in the camper cleaning and the kids were outside playing. Eventually, Kinsley went into her cousin's camper to watch movies with them. I continued to clean up around camp. When it was time to leave, I asked Kinsley to go potty and I was putting her brother Gage in his car seat. This is when I heard the worst sound, her screaming for her life! I looked up from the truck and saw her in the fire pit! Her hands were in the hot ashes and she couldn't get out of the fire pit! I immediately started screaming for help and running to get her. I was about 25 yards from her. Thank goodness, her oldest cousin, Brooke, was near her and grabbed her out of the fire. I got to her, took all her clothes off, and was frozen with fear screaming for help. Her uncle Chris took her from me, and they started hosing her hands off with a water hose to stop the burning. Then my cousin's husband, Jeromy, made an ice bath by cutting the top off of a milk jug. We submerged her hands in the ice bath and wrapped her body in blankets. The other women at camp tried to calm me down enough so I could be with Kinsley.

They put us in my husband's truck and we drove as fast as we could to Eastland Memorial Hospital. I held Kinsley tight, sang songs to her, and asked her to tell me what she wanted Santa to bring her for Christmas to try and keep her mind off the pain and freezing cold water.

When we arrived, we were immediately put in a room and they wrapped her hands and started looking for a way to transport us to Parkland Hospital in Dallas. When they told me they were going to Careflight her to Dallas, I lost it emotionally. I started praying for a miracle. The reality of how bad her injuries were was starting to set in. I felt like I was in a nightmare and it wasn't real.

The doctors determined it to be too windy for a helicopter, so we waited for an ambulance to pick us up and transport us the two hours to Parkland. This is when I realized how amazing God is and how tough that little girl is! She was asking the paramedics about everything inside the ambulance for the two-hour drive.

Upon arrival, we were put in the burn unit. We had surgeons and doctors look at her hands and were told that she had second and third degree burns. They told us it was going to be a long, painful road, but they expected a full recovery. Praise Jesus! She had multiple visitors in the hospital to see her.

The next day was one of the hardest days my husband, Trey, and I have ever experienced! We woke up, they gave Kinsley some oral pain meds, and then they took us to the "Tank." This is where doctors and nurses take patients to do wound care on burn victims. She immediately started throwing up from the medicine when we got in the "Tank." Then, they bathed her, put a mask over her eyes, and started on wound care. We had to watch as they scrubbed and cut on our daughter's hands. It was a living nightmare. She was in so much pain, and she continued to throw up and scream! Trey had to leave the room to compose himself, while I sang songs and held it together for our little girl. When Trey returned, I took my break. While taking a break, I have never had guilt like I did. Guilt for getting the option of taking a break, knowing she couldn't, guilt for not watching her close enough—so much guilt!

When Trey and Kinsley returned to our hospital room, my cousin Britney was there to put a smile on our faces with gifts for Kinsley. She brought her movies and the biggest unicorn you have ever seen. This girl God blessed me

*with lit up and was so happy! You would never know that
she just endured a nightmare two minutes before.*

*In the Parkland Burn Unit, they have a toy room with toys
for the patients. We played a little, but her hands were
wrapped up and she was getting frustrated. They wrapped
her fingers individually so she could still try to use them.
She saw the paint on the shelf and of course she wanted
to use it. We told her that she might not be able to paint
with her fingers in bandages. Boy, did she prove us wrong.
She was able to paint a Christmas tree and ornaments.
She never gave up or got discouraged! I watch that video
and cry because it proves how courageous she is! She is an
inspiration to us all! She never lets it get her down.*

*We went home November 28th, after only one day in the
hospital. My dad and I have been on a long journey for
the past six months taking her to wound care twice a week
at first, then every week, to every other week. She has had
six casts on her left hand, multiple "Tank" and therapy
visits, but we are going strong. She still sleeps in a splint
and does therapy at home. They are predicting that she
will have surgery down the road, but for now, we praise
God for His Healing Hands on hers!*

God has done incredible things in this tiny three-year-old
since the day we barely stood, broken, in the emergency room
of Eastland Memorial Hospital. David and I had hardly been
gone from the ranch ten minutes when we received the call.
We had stopped at Stripes Gas Station, just a few miles down
the road, to get drinks for the ride home, and just entered back
in the truck when we received the call about Kinsley, and flew
out of the parking lot racing to Eastland Memorial Hospital.
David and I both had Eastland Memorial in our phones, to
be proactive in case someone got bit by a snake, and we frantically called them to alert them we were on our way so that

they could be prepared. We used one phone to call the hospital and the other to find directions.

David speeds—a lot—and this time he drove faster than ever. I prayed God's protection on not only our truck but Trey's! I begged and pleaded Him to have mercy on Kinsley and send us all an extra measure of grace, and couldn't imagine the words spoken and not in Trey's truck. So many images were going through my head of what her hands must look like, and I prayed our faith would be bigger than our fear.

When we arrived at the hospital, David quickly parked, and we ran down the sidewalk into the ER. Moments after entering, we saw Tara: broken, distraught, and beside herself, trying to have enough composure to complete the hospital paperwork. I text Lynn, Tara's mom, that I was loving on her girls, as I knew all Lynn wanted was to be able to look into Tara's eyes and tell her it would be ok, even though she wouldn't be sure. That's what all mommies want to do, to say it's ok when it very well may not be.

Not far from where she was doing paperwork were Trey and Kinsley. He was holding her so close, and no doubt he was praying that God would give him her pain. She was covered in blankets, gauze, and tears, and no other word will describe her face other than pitiful. She looked disbelieving, distraught, and confused. Trey's expression was the face of a father who had absolutely no control of the outcome of his only daughter! He was helpless, and his face showed every bit of helplessness.

When David laid eyes on the three of them, he was shattered; we both had the gut-wrenching feeling of knowing nothing we said or did at that moment would make it better. Tara was on the brink of hysteria, crying her eyes out, and we were all five in shock. We waited with them until we found out they were taking her by ambulance, and we then decided to leave and take Trey's truck and hunting gear by their house, with David driving Trey's truck and me driving our rental.

David led and I followed while we drove over ninety miles an hour for two hours due east. I'm not a good driver in my own car, and I'm a horrible driver in a rental going ninety miles per hour while watching my husband recklessly texting and driving in front of me. I was panic-stricken, but God rode with us that day. This was a true showing of His omnipresence and grace as He was in Trey's truck with David, our rental with me, and the ambulance with Kinsley, Tara, and Trey.

What a trooper she has been! She's shown greater strength than some of us all put together. She's endured. We have all learned so much from just watching her walk this out and what a story she has to tell when she gets older. God's used this tiny package to make a big impact, and He used her tiny hands to tug at our hearts. He got our attention and we watched Him work.

I can't begin to fathom the number of people who have voiced prayers for sweet little Rose (Kinsley Rose) as the number has got to be in the thousands. Family prayed, friends of family prayed, churches prayed, colleagues prayed, and probably even strangers prayed. He heard our pleas, and He whispered Healing on her. If you are one of those who prayed, thank you. The entire Taylor family cannot thank you enough. Her blue eyes, ringlets, and bravery have taken many hearts captive. There were months when I would walk into the office, or a campus, and upon sight of me, people would ask, "How's Kinsley?" She captured hearts, including God's (Jehovah Rapha, the Lord your Healer).

The list is long of the things He has done, but her hands went from unrecognizable to the hands you see on the cover of this book, and while skin grafts were mentioned several times, none were needed. I couldn't let the opportunity pass to praise Him and acknowledge Him publicly for what He did! After all, this book is my love letter back to Him, thanking Him for all He's done for me. His love, grace, and compassion never end. I believe 100 percent in my heart that her hands look as great as they do solely because of Him. He loved us enough to hear our prayers, and He loves her enough to lay His Hands on hers.

❤

Lord, there are no words to thank You for the beautiful skin on Kinsley's hands. I pray that when You bring tragedy, that we all can trust You. When You bring gut-wrenching pain and agony that only parents of a suffering child know, may we have enough strength to utter, "I believe."

From my heart to yours:
- When God allows a tragedy to come to your family, does your faith waiver?
- When you have absolutely no control, do you still trust Him?
- When He answers your prayers, do you praise Him?

My prayer for you:
My prayer is that our tears and her pain not be in vain, that someone, somewhere watched our unwavering faith and had faith themselves for what they were facing. Thank You for hearing our prayers. May we never stop praising You!

His healing words to your heart:
"Go back and tell Hezekiah, the ruler of my people, This is what the Lord, the God of your father David, says: I have heard your prayer and seen your tears; I will heal you. On the third day from now you will go up to the temple of the Lord" (2 Kings 20:5).

Chapter 35:
Trusting

"Blessed is she who has believed that the Lord would fulfill his promises to her!" —Luke 1:45

I am still trusting Him as I struggle with daily migraines and challenges with breathing, balance, and memory. While my Dadi was still alive, he called me several times a week to let me know that he prayed for me the night before, and to inquire if today is the day that my coughing had ceased. I can't tell you how much this meant to me and how much I will miss this with him gone. I'm going to take my own best advice and trust that He has this—this is all part of His plan! He has taken such good—no, great—care of me, so why would I not trust Him now? Is such a small thing as my migraine or breathing too difficult for Him? Is this what I think? If He can part the sea and scatter stars in the sky, then my difficulties shouldn't be too difficult for Him.

When I finally surrendered myself to Him, ... I mean,

when I was willing to lose *everything* for Christ's sake, *He came through for me.* He met my needs! I brought all I had to Him and laid it at His feet. This was a time when I knew I would never pick up what I gave Him. He had my word and I had *His*! I trusted Him when I had no other choice, *I trust Him now* and I pray you do also.

Hug His Words in close and your **trust** in Him even closer.

Trust in him at all times, you people, pour out your hearts to him, for God is our refuge. —Psalms 62:8

Completely empty yourself before Him. He cannot fill us if we are already full. He will meet you where you are! He is waiting!

Sometimes we think we are unreachable only to find that He's already got us. Do you feel you can no longer walk? Well, leap! He will be there to catch you. He will have already known you were going to jump. I love that He pursues us!

While He pursues us, pursue His grace.

Sometimes we run while He's chasing us, and all He wants us to do is turn around and fall into His arms.

But when you ask, you must believe and not doubt, because the one who doubts is like a wave of the sea, blown and tossed by the wind. —James 1:6

I need to look to God every day for strength. He is working in me and He will work in you! He has brought me here and He saw me through, and He has not stopped working.

I know I have wasted so many breaths living and doing things on my own, chasing after what was already mine. Don't sell yourself short; He will do the same for you. I just never stopped long enough to rest, catch my breath, then look around and see He was providing the entire time. He was just waiting to leave me *breathless*!

I want to please Him and I want others to know Him, through me, by my life's testimony. It's all about Him.

God, give me the strength for this to happen. Precious Father, thank You for your strength and desire to do what is right. You gave me hope. You brought me through. I will not stop doing for You and Your cause. Thank You for showing me how to breathe in You. Thank You for so many breaths that hurt; they engraved so many things in me, deep in my heart. If I look around me, I will find You. You have never left or forsaken me.

I will take what I have learned from my trials in order to grow and gain strength in Him, for His glory and honor, for it is because of my past that I am who I am today. I am a better person because of what I have gone through. I am thankful that He chose me as one of His vessels to show love and light to others. I am able to show others what He did in me.

❤

God please assure me that You can breathe in me! You can pick me up when I fall; You've done it before. You can whisper hope, air, and peace in me! I know this. God, thank You for my family, friends, and friends that are family who encourage me daily. I will take one breath at a time and trust You for the next! I will put one foot in front of the other, and if I fall, I know You will pick me up! I will never stop trusting and believing in what You can do!

From my heart to yours:

You can do *all* things with His help—anything, everything. So …

- Seek Him! Seek Him first thing in the morning and allow Him to direct your day. *How can you seek Him?*

- Trust Him! Trust that He will provide for you. *What can you give to Him and trust Him with?*

- Allow Him! Allow Him to direct you, guide you, provide for you, strengthen you. *Will you allow Him? What's changed you?*

- Thank Him! Thank Him! Thank Him! (I mean daily! He will not tire of hearing you thank Him.) *What can you thank Him for?*

My prayer for you:

God, may we never grow weak in thanking You! I trusted, I believed that the answer had already been purchased, that I only had to wait patiently. You provided in Your perfect timing, not mine. The beauty in You is that You will do this for my readers. I pray they'll inhale doubt and exhale trust. Thank You, Father, truly thank You for all You've done and all You will do for us. May we never stop believing!

His healing words to your heart:

"He said to her, 'Daughter, your faith has healed you. Go in peace and be freed from your suffering'" (Mark 5:34)

Chapter 36

Migraines and Miracles

There's a God who can bring me up and out. Turning ugly gaping wounds into scars that serve as badges of honor and trophies of the grace of God at work in me. —Bev Murrill

All I wanted was for someone to come alongside me and read me the book of encouragement that I wrote. For them to reach out a hand, to give me the courage to take the next step—the next breath? The past year has been hard, harder than I ever imagined. I never ever thought I would be the person who faced pain every day. I thought the physical changes to my life that I deal with daily were God's plan for me post carbon monoxide poisoning. Boy, was I wrong.

On February 4, 2017, my life changed! Every day since then, my head has hurt. Yes, some days the pain is less, and yes, somedays I'm not nauseous, but I haven't gone one day since without pain, and some days are unbearable. If you are someone who's encouraged me along the way, thank you. Your words mean more than you'll ever know. I trust Him, really I do, but I continually pray for unshakable faith. What scares me most is the unknown, the "what is really happening in there?" feeling.

I woke up with a headache that I knew was a migraine. I've faced many migraines before my poisoning, so I did the normal thing you do with the onset of one and tried to move myself to somewhere calm, quiet, cold, and dark. Day three (Monday) came, and I took off work as I thought if I stayed in this environment, I'd be ok come Tuesday. Had I known that it would go on this long, I would've never missed.

I know for sure a trigger of mine is severe light sensitivity, and I now have rose-tinted migraine glasses to help with the light. These glasses have been a godsend and have helped tremendously. I'm learning to deal with the headache, vertigo, and nausea when it comes, even though some moments are excruciating. Tears come, and some days they sting more than others. I'm still learning to live in His grace, trust His words, and pray I'm strong enough to live out His plan. Every step of every day, I must trust Him. Some days this is unbearably hard, and I find myself doubting and asking if this is His plan. Everyone has a cross to bear, and now I know that migraines are my cross.

Recently, the song "Do It Again" by Elevation Worship broke me! Truly, I wept uncontrollably in the arms of my sister Kimberley. I've put this song on my home screen of my phone and listen to it multiple times a day for strength and encouragement as music has always been a huge part in both my and Taylor's healing. It speaks of God never failing us, that He is faithful and His Promises still stand! He has moved mountains and He will DO IT AGAIN! This has become my migraine anthem, and just like I pray my words will heal and bring encouragement, I am grateful for every word Elevation Worship penned. Their words came when I truly needed them; they pierced my heart with both mercy and grace.

David asked me one night, about forty days in, if we shouldn't call my neurologist and let him know about my migraine. I knew what the doctor had told me seven years ago, in 2010, that there aren't patients quite like us and they really don't know how to treat us, but I would call for David, and I did. I sat in his office on day sixty and read him off a list of things I still struggle with since the last time I saw him (memory issues, balance, breathing, etc.).

He said once again that that's how I am, that's how I'm going to be. He said, "The poisoning changed you, and you are different than before."

I shook my head in agreement and withheld the waiting tears.

"So why are you here today?" he asked.

I told him, "Because I have had a migraine for sixty days."

He wasn't alarmed and voiced, with compassion, "You know I can't fix you."

"Yes, I know, but my husband cares for me deeply," I replied, and I was really there just for David, to make him feel better.

He smiled, then he pointed to my work ID that hung around my neck. "Look what you can do! I know you came from work, it's who you are."

I agreed and flashed a proud smile.

"You're a great writer," he said as he picked up the copy I had given him of our story of the night we were poisoned. He told me to be proud of all the things I can do, which I am.

We talked about medicines I've tried through the years, to no avail, and the possibility of trying something different at the onset of the next migraine, if this one ever leaves. I left his office a little defeated, a little tearful, and felt as if I needed to trust God stronger than I ever had. But mostly I left grateful—grateful for life and breath and a doctor who once again spoke the words of compassion that penetrated my heart a little deeper than before.

❤

Since September 14, 2013, I have looked down at my wedding ring probably thousands of times, and this day was no different. I was working and had been all over the school district and had returned to my office when I looked down at my finger and one of my diamonds was GONE! I asked myself over and over how I could not have noticed this when it happened? In a matter of minutes, I had tons of people searching for a small square-shaped sparkly diamond. After work, we headed to our grandson Carson's baseball game, walked all over the complex, then headed home to dump my purse and check there. I fell asleep thinking of all the places I had been and questioned if I had checked them all.

The next day, I worked like normal, and afterwards I returned a rental car I had after having the dealership search the car like crazy. The following morning David headed to Dallas to have my diamond replaced and waited for two hours for them to open. He called at 10:17 a.m. and said that he had an appointment and couldn't wait any longer, and we agreed that it was ok. I was at work, rushing back and forth from the copier, and felt something in my shoe. I immediately started banging my sandal, thinking it would fall out. Then, I thought, "What if it's the diamond?" and I walked ever so gingerly back to my office, sat down, placed my left foot cross-legged on my right thigh and peeked into my open-toed sandal and THERE IT WAS.

At approximately 10:30 a.m., had the jeweler opened when they said they would, they would have replaced my diamond. Every step for approximately 48 hours, the diamond had gone with me; everywhere I looked it was there. I'm the type of person who, no matter what happens, I feel it's somehow a life lesson and this would prove to be no different.

I had been begging God to show me His plan—show me He still was there—and He had to knock a diamond out of my ring to get my attention. Every step this past year, He's been there and He's still the God of Miracles! My diamonds nestled back in, and so am I. Future plans are to have my diamonds checked twice a year: on Valentine's Day and our wedding anniversary. And just like before, days and breaths continue, some good and some bad, and I'm still trying daily to live out His plan.

❤

Lord, when I doubt or feel hopeless, I speak, "I'm Your girl"—sometimes so softly the words are almost not heard but I know You hear them. Thank You for showing us You are near, even when the healing hasn't come.

From my heart to yours:

- It's easy to trust on day one, but can you trust Him on day 101?

- Even in your darkest hours, when you're feeling alone, can you allow Him to walk with you to let His plan unfold?

My prayer for you:

Taylor asked me if she could write this prayer, and I couldn't wait to see the words that God laid on her heart.

I asked my mom if I could write this prayer, not only because I struggle from migraines myself, but because I wanted to be able to reach out to you, the reader, and pray with you about whatever your struggle is.

Hey Lord, it's me again, as You know I have been praying for You to lead me to the right words to be spoken. Every day we all have struggles, whether it's migraines, addiction,

237

depression, or maybe just everyday life. We all have to go day by day, maybe even step by step, but at the end of the day I pray that it will be worth all the struggle and fight to become who You already know we are. Even in our darkest times, when we think we can't hold on any longer, I pray that we all remember that You, Lord, are already holding us and are there when we fall. You are ready to be our support. Please keep us all close to You, Lord, as we go step by step, fighting through to become who we are meant to be. Thank you, Lord! In Your name, we pray. Amen.

His healing words to your heart:
"For we live by faith, not by sight" (2 Corinthians 5:7).

Chapter 37:
Asking Him into Your Heart

If you declare with your mouth, "Jesus is Lord, "and believe in your heart that God raised him from the dead, you will be saved. " —Romans 10:9

Don't close this book and let my story end without the confirmation of knowing you're going to Heaven. We don't know how long He will tarry, and the time is now to make this possible.

It's simple, let me show you how…

We are all sinners.

> For all have sinned and fall short
> of the *glory* of God. —Romans 3:23

"Sinned" means that we have missed the mark. When we lie, hate, lust or gossip, we have missed the standard God has set for us.

The penalty for sin is death.

> For the wages of sin is death, but the gift of God is *eternal life* in Christ Jesus our Lord. —Romans 6:23

The Bible tells us that by sinning we have earned death, and we deserve total separation from God forever.

Christ died for you.

> But God demonstrates his own *love* for us in this: While we were still sinners, Christ died for us. —Romans 5:8

Christ took the penalty we deserved for sin, placed it upon Himself, and died in our place. Three days later, He came back to life to prove that sin and death had been conquered and that His claim to be God were true.

You can be saved through faith in Christ.

> For it is by *grace* you have been *saved*, through faith·and this is not from yourselves, it is the *gift* of God·not by works, so that no one can boast. —Ephesians 2:8–9

Isn't that encouraging? *Faith means trust.* What must you trust Christ for? You must depend on Him alone to forgive you and to give you eternal life. *It is His gift.*

Would you like to tell God you are trusting Jesus Christ as your Savior? If you would, why not pray right now and tell God you are trusting His Son? (It's not the prayer that saves;

it's trusting Jesus Christ. Prayer is simply how you tell God what you're doing.)

"Dear God, I know I'm a sinner. I know my sin deserves to be punished. I *believe* Jesus Christ died for me and rose from the grave. I *trust* Jesus Christ alone as my Savior. Thank You for the forgiveness and everlasting life I now have. In Jesus' Name, Amen."

❤

From my heart to yours:

If you just prayed and asked Jesus into your heart, it's the best decision you'll ever make, and I'm so proud of you! I'd love to know so I can pray for you during this new journey. Email me at shelley@shelleytaylor.net. Iron sharpens iron, so find a church near you and get connected.

My prayer for you:

Lord, You know I'm thrilled for the people who have come to know You by You making this book possible. I believe this is the most important decision they can ever make. Lord, I pray You will connect with them and connect them to a church where they can grow the seeds that have been planted in their hearts. I am forever grateful that you came alongside me and walked my journey with me and *With My Last Breath, I'd Say I Love You.*

His healing words to your heart—benediction:

"The Lord bless you and keep you; the Lord make his face shine on you and be gracious to you; the Lord turn His face toward you and give you peace" (Numbers 6:24–26).

Love Letters

To Mother:

Standing beside your bed in hospice, watching you fade, I was numb. I carry a lot of numbness still, the same that I have felt most of my life and that which was magnified after you died. Numb to me always felt better than pain. Sometimes I needed you more than I needed my next heartbeat, my next breath. The peace of not having a mother still hasn't come, but God's grace continues. I will continue to abide in it.

I have wondered for years what I would say in this letter to you, and I'm writing it and still not sure. All I know to say is, "All I ever wanted you to do was love me." Simply that. "I feel as if you never really could and you didn't, and I forgive you." I will never understand how you could choose drugs and alcohol over your children and cause irreparable pain and heartache. It is not for me to understand. God so graciously sent me family and friends that filled in the gap and for that I am grateful. Life carried on in your absence and I have no regrets. **I am loved and *With My Last Breath, I'd Say I Love You.***

To Dadi:

Dadi, I'm sitting here writing this while watching and listening to you take your last few breaths. We've been here for days listening to you breathe. I even woke in the night and heard your breath, and when the room finally goes silent, we will cry. I can't help but ponder that you are the reason I have breath; you gave me life, and I *live*. You prayed for me and loved me with an unconditional love and no matter what I did, what I said, you loved me! Thank you for interceding for me during all my broken years. You helped me become whole. You took me broken and laid me at the Father's feet when I didn't have the strength to take myself. You plead to God for me. He heard your prayers and He sent me into the arms of David and linked our hands and hearts.

I only hope that I can pray for Taylor like you have prayed for me. Let go, Dadi, give up the fight. You are our hero, our King on earth. I am forever grateful that God chose you to be my Dadi. He knew just what I would need and then He created you. Go see, Mother. It's time, she's waiting. Let go of my hand and grab Jesus'. Just a few more steps in your journey—keep going, don't look back. We will all be fine. Look for the light, Dadi, look for the light. The last thing you ever have to do for me is give me your breath. Dadi, you have prayed for my coughing and breathing every night since we were poisoned … give me your breath. **Thank you, Dadi. I love you!**

To David:

I've tried so many times to write this to you, and no words seem appropriate. Sometimes I'm a better "*shower*" than "*teller*," and I can only hope that I have shown you my love for you. No one has ever loved me and cared for me like you.

You love my daughter, you snuggle me, you compliment me, you kiss me, you hold my hand, and you hold me. You take care of me, you love the little things that matter to me, and you're the first voice I hear in the mornings and the last I hear before we sleep. You check on me during the day, you share conversation with me, you dine with me, you laugh at me, you laugh with me, you worship with me, and you share your babies and grandbabies with me. You and I can do nothing and it feels like everything. You give me hope, you gave me *life* and *love* and *breath* and *purpose*, and you tell me you love me, because you do.

I know I was put on this earth to love you and give you purpose. I was meant to share my last chapter by your side, in your arms and in your heart. I want you spoiled and happy, and I want to nestle into all your broken places. I couldn't love you more, and He has blessed me more than I ever dreamed, for which I am eternally grateful. The birth of our relationship was the epitome of me needing to stop holding on and just be held. Thank you for holding me. Sometimes our battles spill us into who He meant us to be all along, and I am proof of that. **There are not enough words to tell you how much I love you!**

The night before we were married, I wrote this for David:

His deeply lined eyes show not only countless years of wisdom, but the often times he is mused by ordinary life moments that he has not only experienced but shared, and at the time of this writing I find myself an honored recipient. At this moment, I am captivated by his caring eyes, longing smile, moral character, and the repetitiveness of his enduring touch, and can't help but feel these things are intoxicating. No one knows the intimacy of what he and I have shared. Years have passed since he has allowed his heart to be thread to another in such a trusting way.

[I am] truly honored, thankful, and grateful to our God above to have received such a blessing as He has bestowed me and promised me if only I would trust Him. I will not only give my life, but I will embark with him in ordinary moments given extraordinary meanings and breaths. I will take the ocean full of tears that I cried and turn them into ink to record the moments we share turned magical by two beating hearts with an unending reason to once again celebrate life as a union with not only ourselves but our children. Every moment matters, the ones that break

us and the ones that make us. I took Dadi out to lunch one day and read him a list of qualities that a man would have to meet for me to marry him. David met them all! I can mark Dadi seeing me happy off my "bucket list."

The following is what I read David at our wedding: "Wow!" And you, thank you for being my soft place to fall. But thank you for picking me up! Most of all, thank you for being my rock! I know I leaned on you hard and I made you be strong for the both of us. I hope I have shown you how to trust again, not only in me and in things, but in *Him*! And *faith*, I hope I have shown you *faith, in yourself, in God and in me.* **I *never* stopped believing! I love you, baby!"**

To my baby girl, Taylor:

The following is what I read Taylor at my wedding to David: *"To you, little girl: All the years that I supported you, making you strong enough to stand on your own, I never knew in return I was making you strong enough to support me! Thank you for being there for me, for picking me up when I fell (literally). God paid that forward and you saw me trust Him, with an incredible amount of faith, and then you did the same. You trusted in Him and He came through for you.* **I love you, baby girl!"**

What a huge blessing you received in Keifer. I can still remember the first time you showed me his picture and you said, "Mom, isn't he so cute?" I bet you looked at that picture a zillion times. I am so thankful God sent Keifer to show you love, life, and God's love for you. Keifer encouraged you to look up in the midst of our storm. God never left your side, sweetie; He just inserted Keifer in between you and Him. I taught you how to love like I do, with everything you have. It's risky, but it feels amazing. When you receive the same kind of love back, it is breathtaking and it's exactly what I wanted for you. That's what I see in Keifer—that kind of love. He loves you like I wanted you to be loved. I pray for y'all constantly. I love y'all dearly and welcome him into our family with open arms. You are as beautiful as the ring he gave you. Truly you realized why no one else worked out; God had a plan. He is faithful when we trust Him and let His plan unfold, in His timing.

I am so proud of you, and I can't even find the words to tell you how proud I am. You never dreamed you would be an American Sign Language (ASL) interpreter. Look how far you've come! You took all your compassion and put it into a career, and you will bless people without a doubt. God had a plan for your creativeness. It was absolutely priceless when Ms. Cobb called me and said, "I'll never get your daughter. I'll never get how she cannot even spell her own name on paper, but can fingerspell it accurately."

"She gets it!" I said. "She's the Barbie with the head on backwards." We laughed and almost cried because we were so proud of you. It's not a coincidence that Ms. Cobb was the first ASL teacher we hired in Mansfield ISD, then later left and was your professor in college. You were blessed to have her both places and have her skills, love and compassion. God truly orchestrates things if we let Him. I can't imagine what she felt when she watched you walk across that stage, but I think I felt the same feelings.

I can't believe that I had a part in creating *you*! I am one proud mama. Just remembering how I almost lost you at birth and how sick you were at six weeks old and all the challenges you've faced and where you've come is almost more than I can take in. I couldn't have done everything you've done. You have loved me when I felt as if I didn't deserve being loved. You have prayed for me, encouraged me, laughed with me, and you've been an incredible daughter to walk beside. Everything that I wanted for my mother and me is exactly what I hope I can give you. I can't wait to walk the rest of this journey out with you. **I'll never be able to tell you how much I love you!**

To our children:

Words from our wedding: "Thank you for loving me and thank you for letting me love you! Thank you for being the family I wanted and needed! Thank you for letting me share your dad, your spouses, and your babies. **I love y'all!**"

So much has happened during the years I've loved y'all: death, life, sickness, health, love, birth, adoption. I am honored to have collected breaths and birthday candles with you and your littles. I've loved being "Honey." Thank you for allowing me to spoil your dad; we have enjoyed the most incredible journey, and you all have made it even more special. Neither of us could have known that we would spend our final chapter together, and I could've never written this happily ever after for us. I will tell you this: I prayed so many prayers for your dad, not knowing it was he I was praying for. I love you like you were mine, and I love your littles and spouses no different than I do you. God is blessing me through each of you, and each of you is special and unique to me—and I love it! Thank you for loving me just as I am. I hope I please you more than I fail you, but I'm thankful for grace when I don't. **I love you all, "Honey."**

To Nanny (David's mother):

You told me one day, "I don't know why God keeps me around so long." My response: "For me!" You have lived a plentiful ninety-one years, and I know your days are decreasing. You have said things to me sweeter than I could've ever imagined, you have been a true encourager for me regarding my book and I know God puts us in the sweetest of places to receive His grace. I wouldn't trade anything for just sitting here watching you sleep. I hope I never forget all the times you and I shared conversation and coffee out of your precious percolator. I promise always to keep it nestled close by and will always think of you when I use it. I am forever grateful for our relationship. Thank you, David, for sharing her with me. I am beyond blessed to have you both. **I love you, Nanny!**[4]

To my sisters:

We have laughed together and cried together and laughed until we cried, together. We have been united by births, sickness and disease, and deaths. We have been through a lot. We share a deep history, and the blood that flows through many. *I would not be breathing breaths or feeling my heart beat at this moment if not for the two of you.* So many days and moments you breathed life and love in me. You were both so instrumental in Him rescuing me. He heard your prayers and learned your voices. God sent compassion, mercy, and grace through both of you, and words have not yet come to thank you and honor you for your love! **I love you both deeply!**

To my friends:

You can't possibly know how much your love and support has meant to me all these years. To those who prayed, He heard you. To those who held my hand, the warmth was incredible—don't let go. (Some of you had to drag me just to

---

4 I wrote this while sitting at the hospital with her after she broke her hip, not long before we would lose her.

take that first small step, and you'll never know how much I appreciate it.) Thank you for loving me when I was unlovable and showing me unconditional love on so many days that I was undeserving. Thank you to each of you who drug me to the final written word; I'm beyond blessed to have you love me so deeply! This book wouldn't have been possible without your love and prayers. **I love you muches!**

To my brain injury community:

Thank you for sharing love, hope and determination with me daily! To Amy Zellmer, author of *Surviving Brain Injury: Stories of Strength and Inspiration, and Life with a Traumatic Brain Injury: Finding the Road Back to Normal,* thank you for including our TBI story and thank you for your TBI Tribe and your enormous passion for all of us. Donna O'Donnell Figurski, and your Brain Injury Radio Network, **thank you for allowing us to be on your panel and sharing our story.** And to Cyndi Feasel for writing *After the Cheering Stops: An NFL wife's story of concussion, loss and the faith that saw her through* and your deep compassion to prevent brain injuries. To the thousands of hospitals, rehabs, ministries, etc. that provide brain injury awareness, **thank you for being a shadow to my courage and a welcoming face at each day's finish line.** While these are not the paths we picked for ourselves, we are all in this together and it's truly your encouragement that softens the blows. I hope I have paid forward some of your cheers. May you continue each day with hope and healing. **I love you all.**

To my readers:

Writing changed my life, my lifestyle, my complete being.

It changed who I was, who I would be, and the result I wanted to see in not only myself but others, you included. I am so grateful that God has used my writing to change others' lives. My hope will always be, if I write today, it may change someone's tomorrow. *I couldn't be more humbled that He's penned hope in others' lives by penning mine.* He spilled ink on me, and I will pay it forward.

To the precious lady that I received a message from in total desperation, who told me you read some of my writing and it made you decide to live, you are why I write, and others just like you! Truly our lives changed that day. I felt purpose, I was completely overwhelmed, and I found myself speechless as spoken words froze mine. My breaths counted that day, and your breaths continue because I followed my purpose and wrote. God intervened with the words He gave me. Divine intervention at its finest! God won that day, and all the days forward. We will forever have a connection. My writing will always be not only for me, but for those who will read what I write. To know that what I wrote made a difference to someone means I will never step away from the keyboard and never put down the pen. If I silence what's inside, what if it's exactly what you need to hear? That day it was! Words written, mixed with tears, made for two lives changed forever. *Words matter, and my heart's desire is that your life was changed.*

To myself:

I was stronger than I thought. I wish I had written down all the places where I had written this book: the little house on Brown Street, Xavier's, our new home, David's truck, Nocona around the table and propped up on the front porch, Cisco in Trey and Tara's camper and around the campfire, DFW National Cemetery, lunch hours in the parking lot of work and the Methodist church, voice texts driving numerous places,

Puerto Vallarta on the plane and listening to the ocean waves, Fredericksburg, Nanny's hospital room, Nanny's house, Kim's home in Kingsland, and her new home in Corpus Christi, just to name a few. I am so pleased with myself for submitting to Him; it sincerely paid off. I have so many hopes for this book, dreams of helping and providing hope to *those recovering, those still fighting*, and *those just breathing*. There were so many times, numerous times, that I didn't think it was possible to finish after being poisoned. I thought the task was just too great. Well, it was possible! God had a plan, and I am so grateful He let me be the vessel to carry it out. If we surrender to Him and let Him use us, He will. It's simple—*just surrender.*

From my heart to yours:

- What would you say with your *last breath*?

- Who can you write a *love letter* to? Start with writing one to yourself.

My prayer for you:

Whether you write to someone you've loved and lost, or loved and are still loving, write to someone, share your heart, share you, and share what you love about them. Words escape me for what I feel that you took the time to read my love letter. I hope you are stronger than the first time my book sat in your hands and you have a greater sense of accomplishment for what you can do and who you are. I pray the challenge of some of your breaths has been lessened. I am stronger because of the words I wrote, and I have seen healing with every chapter. For the words that were left unwritten, I pray He will continue His healing. Countless years, days, and hours have been poured into these pages, and my desire is that something I've said, something I've lived, resonated enough with you to touch your heart. I hope I have been a light in your darkness, and if you need someone in your corner fueling your spark, I'm here for you. I have prayed so many prayers for you along the way, and it is my prayer that you will pray for me, my continued healing, and those I love. **I am forever grateful and *With My Last Breath, I'd Say I Love You.***

His healing words to your heart:

"Love is patient, love is kind. It does not envy, it does not boast, it is not proud. It does not dishonor others, it is not self-seeking, it is not easily angered, it keeps no record of wrongs. Love does not delight in evil but rejoices with the truth. It always protects, always trusts, always hopes, always perseveres. *Love never fails*" (1 Corinthians 13:4–8, emphasis added).